▼

▼
Black Elk

▼

▼

Black Elk
Holy Man
of the Oglala

by Michael F. Steltenkamp

University of Oklahoma Press : Norman and London

By Michael F. Steltenkamp

The Sacred Vision: Native American Religion and Its Practice Today (Ramsey, N.J., 1982)
Black Elk: Holy Man of the Oglala (Norman, 1993)

Unless otherwise indicated, all photographs are from the author's collection. Maps are by Gilbert Cymbalist.

Text design is by Cathy Imboden.

Steltenkamp, Michael F.
    Black Elk, holy man of the Oglala / by Michael F. Steltenkamp.
        p. cm.
    Includes bibliographical references (p.   ) and index.
    ISBN 0-8061-2541-1 (alk. paper)
    1. Black Elk, 1863–1950. 2. Oglala Indians—Biography.
3. Oglala Indians—Religion and mythology. 4. Ogala
Indians—Missions. I. Title
    E99.03B538   1993   93-22089
    973'.04975—dc20   CIP

Dedicated to the memory of
my grandmother, Lucy Looks Twice,
my mother, Julia Antoinette Steltenkamp,
and all Good Ones of Wakan Tanka.

▼

▼

Contents

Illustrations

Figures

Maps

▼

▼

Preface

A friend who lived some distance out in the country needed a ride home, so I agreed to take him. He came from a traditional Lakota background.[1] In fact, English was his second language. Driving over dry roads on the Pine Ridge Indian Reservation in ninety-degree weather would make us thirsty, we knew, so before setting out, we bought a can of soda. As we drove along, we emptied the can, and my friend turned toward his window, then stopped: "Mind if I throw this out?"

The question took me by surprise. Here was a young man whose usual behavior reminded me of the prereservation period, when the Plains were free of twentieth-century pollution. A rare moment had presented itself, so I responded by asking: "Did you ever see the television commercial that showed an Indian man in buckskin paddling down a river? When he landed, someone threw trash at his feet, and the Indian man was pictured with a tear on his cheek?" Pensive for a few moments, my friend answered, "Yeah, what's *he* crying about?"

"The commercial seemed to be showing that years ago, before settlers came to America, someone could paddle down a river and not see any trash lying around at all. And if an Indian from a long time ago saw how polluted America had become, he would cry." That was the point of the television commercial as I understood it.

I awaited my friend's reaction. He did not reply immediately; instead, he was taken up in thought. With a look of bewilderment, and with no inflection in his voice, he asked: "You mean I'm not supposed to throw this can out the window?"

I told him I would throw it away when I got home, and he set it on the seat between us.

The matter was closed, but my friend seemed perplexed by the decision. If I wanted to carry an empty soda can back home with me, fine—but doing so was not the choice my friend would have made. He could not identify with his television counterpart. Never again would I view that commercial with my same, previously unchallenged assumptions.

My experience illustrates a larger issue that this work addresses: how the legacy of stereotypes we have inherited obscures the flesh-and-blood individuals who are Native people. I pursue this issue by focusing on the life of Black Elk, a "holy man of the Oglala Sioux," who has been characterized in ways that have spawned numerous images of the Indian world that are not entirely accurate (Neihardt 1972). His life story can shed light on the larger, more complex social system within which he lived (Bourguignon 1979:19). Black Elk can tell us much about the Lakota world view, and it is his story, his special role in the panorama of Indian culture, that the rest of these pages address. In the process, far more than just one man's life will be better understood.

When Thomas Mails persuaded "ceremonial chief" Frank Fools Crow to relate his life experiences (1979), readers of that biography met a man who enjoyed unique genealogical, political, and religious prominence among the Lakota.

Besides addressing the United Nations General Assembly during the 1970s on behalf of Indian America, this elder statesman acquired prestige and notoriety among his people as the repository of sacred knowledge. At first unwilling to discuss this information, he relented only when Mails told him that the revered Black Elk, an uncle to Fools Crow, had recounted his own life history years earlier. The fact that Black Elk had chosen this course demanded that Fools Crow reconsider his own position. After all, even for Fools Crow, Black Elk was a beacon. His stature, Fools Crow knew, dwarfed that of all modern religious practitioners, including Fools Crow himself (from whom many others were taking their cue). What Fools Crow did not know was that Black Elk was perhaps the best known of all American Indians.

Black Elk's life and thought were first brought to the public forum in 1932 through the poetic craftsmanship of John Neihardt.[2] After this initial introduction, Joseph Epes Brown transmitted the holy man's knowledge of Lakota religious tradition in a work entitled *The Sacred Pipe* (1953). The numerous reprints of both books (in America and Europe) attest to the appeal of what Black Elk had to say.

Neihardt and Brown portrayed him as a man living in his memories of prereservation life. Born when buffalo was still the staple of Plains tribes, he shared in the victory of Little Big Horn (1876) and witnessed the heartbreak of Wounded Knee (1890). Throughout these summer and winter years, Black Elk grew into manhood. As DeMallie has noted (1984a:124), however, Neihardt and Brown both erred by depicting him solely as a nineteenth-century figure.

Consisting largely of first-person narratives, *Black Elk Speaks* portrayed Sioux life as it existed during the latter half of the 1800s. Like other works of its kind, the biography recounts boyhood memories and early adult experiences, village and family life, religious ritual, and sober reflection. Historical figures such as Crazy Horse, Buffalo Bill Cody, and George Armstrong Custer all come alive in the powerful simplicity of Black Elk's account.

Except for an incident reported in the postscript, *Black Elk Speaks* restricts itself to the downfall of the Sioux as a self-sufficient people. Prereservation days are portrayed as generally carefree times, the Indian victory at Little Big Horn becomes a prelude to reservation confinement, and the 1890 massacre at Wounded Knee is shown as a coup de grace to an entire way of life. His dream, Black Elk said, died with those who fell in this final conflict. In effect, Neihardt casts the holy man in the role of spokesman for all Lakota, if not all Indian people. Dee Brown continued this image when he used Black Elk's grim reflection on the demise of the Sioux as a conclusion for his 1970 best-seller *Bury My Heart at Wounded Knee.*

In *Black Elk Speaks,* the holy man prays to Wakan Tanka (Great Spirit), "Maybe the last time on this earth, I recall the great vision you sent me" (233).[3] He is presented as a very old man, nearly blind, who might well pass away at any moment. That Black Elk experienced so much personal hurt along with his people only adds greater emotional impact to the closing pages of this book. "Noble savage" and "vanishing American" motifs reverberate throughout the final passages.[4]

Sixteen years after Neihardt wrote of Black Elk in this fashion, however, Joseph Epes Brown came upon the very same man and found him still very much alive! Brown asked Black Elk to describe the seven rites of the Oglala Sioux—traditional religious ceremonies belonging to the earlier period but practiced irregularly in recent times. With the publication in 1953 of *The Sacred Pipe,* the holy man's knowledge of ritual was brought to the fore. Once again, readers were understandably touched by what Black Elk had to say.

In sum, the two books portray Black Elk and the social

institutions he so cherished as paralyzed victims of Western subjugation. Doomed to live out his years as a relic of the past and prisoner of irreconcilably foreign ways, the holy man (and his people) becomes an object of pity. Readers are left to conclude that Black Elk lived his first thirty years productively and endured his last sixty tearfully.

Nothing was known of Black Elk's life for the forty years not treated by Neihardt, and except for Brown's eight-month visit in the winter of 1947–48, nothing is known of Black Elk's last twenty years. Essentially, then, sixty years of the man's life are unaccounted for, and readers are left to wonder whether Black Elk participated at all in the twentieth-century reservation world (fifty years of which he knew).

Brown's 1971 preface to *The Sacred Pipe* rightly suggested that what so far has been revealed in the two books on Black Elk only "raises the question as to who, in fact, Black Elk really was" (xiii). Roger Dunsmore (1977) raised the same question, insisting that one of the principal tasks of anthropologists is to understand how people such as Black Elk made sense of the disastrous encounter between Oglala culture and the invading white culture (if indeed they did). Such concerns no doubt have confronted most readers of the moving, though enigmatic, commentaries ascribed to the man in either book. Perhaps readers wonder if people like Black Elk exist any more, or if in fact they ever did exist.

So evocative is Black Elk's characterization that it has been expropriated and utilized on behalf of diverse forms of special pleading. Environmental activists, Indian militants, anthropologists, historians, religionists, students of Americana, and others have gleaned from Black Elk passages that bolster or refute whatever conventional Native theme they choose because, it appears, his representation has become *the* conventional stereotype par excellence.[5] Those aware of this larger frame of reference are thus con-

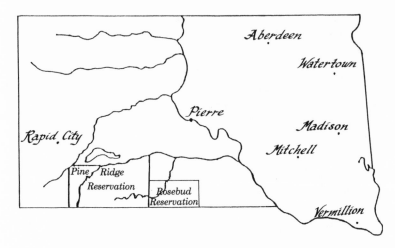

Map 1. South Dakota, showing the Pine Ridge and Rosebud
reservations.

fronted with the task of separating the wheat from the chaff—
discerning whether Black Elk was a kind of "modal man"
of the Sioux, a mystic, or a myth.

A certain irony accompanies the Neihardt-Brown portrayal in that their Black Elk elicits admiration from readers, even though his story represents a kind of personal and
societal death-rattle. Cultural forms after Wounded Knee
are shown to be by-products of a lifeless resignation to non-
Indian ways that the holy man was forced to endure. Many
readers perhaps assumed that Black Elk's life typified the
experience of the Oglala people (and others) on their mark-
erless path from nomadic times to sedentary living. However, only by analyzing the man's *entire* life, within the
constraints of the nineteenth- *and* twentieth-century Lakota
milieu, can we attempt cross-cultural comparisons or interpret Black Elk's socialization and world view.

When I assumed a teaching position on the Pine Ridge
Reservation, I was on the very same terrain that had been

home to the holy man for most of his life (see map 1). Joseph Epes Brown had been one of my college instructors just the year before, so I was eager to seek out (as he had done) living custodians of ancient ways and perhaps learn more about the famous holy man himself.

After only a short time, however, I learned to my great astonishment that Black Elk's prestige in the reservation community was not attributable to the popularity of his two books. Prestige he had, but it was the result of his very active involvement with priests in establishing Catholicism among his people. Older persons remembered him as "Nick" Black Elk, and most knew little (if anything) about the two books based on his life and thought. Those who were familiar with the literature thought it was the work of Nick's son Ben.[6]

Neihardt made passing reference to Black Elk as a preacher in his introduction (*BES*, x) but concentrated his attention on the man's role as a traditional holy man *(wicasa wakan)* of the Lakota. In describing Black Elk only as "a kind of a preacher," Neihardt left the most significant portion of the man's life story unreported.[7] To my amazement, I learned that Black Elk had preached Christian doctrine to his people for the greater part of his life and that he had been formally invested with the office of catechist.

Readers of *The Sacred Pipe* initially are made aware of Black Elk's familiarity with Christianity but are not told its full implications. The simplicity of his testimony is easily glossed over when juxtaposed with the wealth of Lakota religious tradition he proceeds to relate. The holy man is quoted in Brown's 1971 preface as saying: "We have been told by the white man, or at least by those who are Christian, that God sent to men his son, who would restore order and peace upon the earth; and we have been told that Jesus the Christ was crucified, but that he shall come again at the Last Judgment, the end of this world or cycle. *This I understand and know it is true*" (xix, italics added). This creed seems to have been read in terms of Black Elk's being only superficially acquainted with Christian doctrine. As I later learned, much more was involved.

When Ben Black Elk died in February 1973, and as I sang with the Lakota choir at his burial, I felt a great loss. Now that Ben was gone, I thought, a direct family link with the Oglala holy man could no longer be made. The child of so venerable a parent as Nick Black Elk might have shed some light on the questions raised by the old Sioux patriarch. I had barely known Ben, and now he was dead. The book seemed closed on Nick Black Elk's life, and further illumination seemed left pretty much to anyone's speculation.[8]

Such were my feelings when just three months after Ben's funeral, I happened to meet an *unci* (grandmother) who was seated on a bench in front of the Holy Rosary Mission.[9] I asked her if she perhaps had attended school at the mission years earlier, when only one building served as the entire educational complex. The question prompted her to take a long look at the grounds and seemed to take her back many years to another time and another style of life. Her wrinkled face bespoke a glimmer of nostalgia as she replied: "When I was just a little girl, I came to school here, and so did my brother Ben. Since he passed away, this school dedicated its yearbook to his memory." This is how I met Lucy, Black Elk's only surviving child.

We spoke awhile, and I asked if I might visit her someday. I explained that I was a teacher at the Red Cloud Indian High School and was attempting to relate her father's story to the students. I felt that she might be able to help me understand more deeply just who her father was.

Lucy said she would be happy to explain as much as she could about her father and that I could visit her whenever I wished. We shook hands and parted until two weeks later, when the spring rains had ceased and country roads permitted passage.

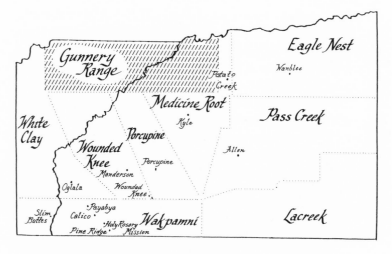

Map. 2. Pine Ridge Reservation, with districts and villages.

Lucy's home was an old log house roughly four miles north of Manderson, South Dakota, a small town on the Pine Ridge Reservation (see map 2). When I arrived for our first meeting, Lucy suggested we sit under a shelter of pine boughs that her husband, Leo, had constructed. There we could speak uninterrupted by the smaller grandchildren who were playing around the house.[10]

As I interviewed her, I based my questions on material drawn from *Black Elk Speaks* and *The Sacred Pipe*. Lucy brought me up short by saying she had never read either book and that she knew very little about her father's life as a young man. The more I referred to the books, the more I realized Lucy had other things on her mind. I was beginning to think she did not really wish to have me visit or to ask questions about anything. Finally, sensing our encounter would soon be over, I asked if there was anything she felt should be known about her father that was not already known to people.

It was then I learned of a dream Lucy had carried with her

ever since her father's death. For years she had waited to have her father's life fully recorded. So far, it had not been. So far, it had been told only partially by John Neihardt, and *The Sacred Pipe* did not capture what she felt was most significant. Moreover, Lucy was disappointed that her father was now being misunderstood and that people were using the material from his books in a way he never intended.

I told Lucy of my desire to learn what she had to say and of my willingness to help put together a conclusive biography of her father. At the time, I little realized what this task would entail. I corresponded with Joseph Epes Brown during this period, and his words gave additional incentive to my visits with Lucy over the next few years. He wrote: "I have felt it improper that this phase of his life was never presented either by Neihardt or indeed by myself. I suppose somehow it was thought this Christian participation compromised his 'Indianness,' but I do not see it this way and think it time that the record was set straight."

Brown suggested that the record be set straight, and it was clearly Lucy's intention throughout the course of my relationship with her to do just that. She had long desired to undertake such a project and, from that time on, looked forward to my visits. In her declining years, Lucy knew that not much time remained for her to fulfill the vision of relating her father's life story.

After several years of interviews, visits, and correspondence, I read to Lucy my translating, transcribing, compiling, editing, interpreting, and polishing—a methodological luxury her father (and other Native consultants, I am sure) did not enjoy. She was quite satisfied with our collaborative effort, and I was pleased to have mediated the preparation of a written text that had included many disparate, and sometimes disconnected, means of inquiry (i.e., taping sessions, planned and unplanned visits, solicited and unsolicited letters, family gatherings, and chance meetings).

Other consultants upon whom this work depends knew

Black Elk personally. Most of his intimates were either long
dead, however, or seriously infirm, so necessity required
my attending to a senior generation that was fast slipping
away. It was within their camp that the substance of Black
Elk's life and thought was best preserved.

Her brother Ben was now gone, and Lucy's health was
not good. The Neihardt-Brown portrait of her father was,
these long years after his death, being invoked by people
(both extended-family members and outsiders) who did
not really know him. In turn, these people were espousing
social actions, religious sentiments, and practices she
knew her father would not so readily affirm.[11] Hence, I
was eager to learn more about Black Elk's life and thought,
and Lucy was long ready to pass on what previously had
been left unreported.[12] In addition to being a biography of
Black Elk from the viewpoint of his daughter and friends,
this inquiry will illuminate corners of the Lakota world
that have heretofore been shadowy or indeed misrepresented.

Stated more directly, the tendency has been to compart-
mentalize Black Elk's life and thought into an era untainted
by non-Indian social or religious currents. Such a tack is,
quite simply, easier to pursue, since it avoids having to
analyze disparate influences that reside beyond the Lakota
world. The fact remains, however, that the holy man lived
well beyond the Wounded Knee tragedy, and he did so with
much vitality. Black Elk's life goes beyond the neat construct of total nativism on the one hand, or complete ab-
sorption of Western ways on the other. His biography is not
a profile in syncretism but is, rather, an example of reflexive adjustment to new cultural landscapes that previously
had not been explored.

The conventional assumption regarding Lakota history
is that chameleonlike, a pastel world changed to moribund
gray in the years after Wounded Knee. A "people's dream"
had died, and their once-vital lifeblood clotted with each

passing year. Poverty and depression hung heavily upon the now-hunched shoulders of a proud "warrior society," and the already-fading pulse of a people in despair lessened more and more. A grim and spectral reality was this Indian culture, and it very much clashed with an America whose global supremacy was beginning to emerge.

Before and after the massacre of Wounded Knee in 1890, many Lakota indeed suffered a malaise of spirit over several decades that certainly took its toll on their morale. And yet, the holy man lived—animatedly, serenely, lovingly, spiritually—through all of it. The contention of this work is not to disprove the anomic realities that have characterized so much of the reservation period but rather to explain how persons like Black Elk were able to face such odds and come to terms with them. The following pages seek to understand how a stereotypical Plains medicine man of the nineteenth century could experience so many perturbations of life-style, meaningfully integrate new patterns of activity, and live out his days more or less happily.

Here is the story of a now-famous medicine man whose life was altered in a dramatic encounter at the deathbed of a dying child. A ritual specialist from one religious tradition confronted an "intrusive other," and life was never again quite the same. Depending upon one's point of view, such was Black Elk's fated destiny, fortuitous chance, bad luck, or providential call. Whatever perspective one adopts on this chapter of the man's life, it needs to be understood that what seems a radically abrupt break with tradition is, at its core, an unfolding of reality that the holy man was predisposed to cope with, comprehend, assimilate, and address with considerable satisfaction. Plains culture itself was the source of this preadaptation.

Rapid settlement of the West eliminated many of the identifiable features of prereservation life. These features truly had a substance of their own, and their loss can only be imagined by we who are removed from those times and places. Nonetheless, by examining Black Elk's life, we can appreciate Lakota experience from perspectives that heretofore have been overlooked. And so, this biography does not just offer some telling facts about one man's life. It provides new glimpses of how, in fact, an entire group carried on against challenges that are today still menacing.

Many years have elapsed since the writing of this biography was first undertaken. Apart from the Pine Ridge residents quoted in this book, there are numerous others who in some way helped see it through to completion. I acknowledge their special, unsung contribution, and my heart shakes hands with theirs. Moreover, I am especially grateful to Raymond J. DeMallie of Indiana University, whose scholarship set standards to emulate and whose assistance produced better revisions. Similarly, Charles Cleland, Robert McKinley, John McKinney, and Charles Morrison of Michigan State University and Daniel J. Gelo of the University of Texas at San Antonio provided helpful suggestions and clarifications. Gilbert Cymbalist and Randy Lukasiewicz contributed important supplementary material, as did Mark G. Thiel of Marquette University's Archives, and the late F. W. Thomsen of Dana College. Jesuit Fathers Raymond Bucko, Bernard Fagan, Michael Flecky, Paul Manhart, Paul Prucha, Ronald Seminara, John Staudenmaier, Paul Steinmetz, Glen Welshons, and Theodore Zuern offered helpful perspectives on the history of the Lakota. Finally, gratitude is extended to John Drayton from the University of Oklahoma Press, whose role as editor was eclipsed only by his role as friend.

MICHAEL F. STELTENKAMP
Bay Mills Reservation, Michigan

▼

▼

Black Elk

▼

chapter one

▼

Lakota Culture

In order to understand Black Elk's later life, it is necessary to understand the cultural system within which he was born and the social organization with which he was familiar. Before achieving notoriety as an individual, the holy man was an anonymous participant in Native American Plains life, as that life was conventionally defined by his particular group. These initial pages flesh out the identity of a people whose very name has elicited controversy and confusion. By addressing this issue of name, and then the people's social configuration and history, this chapter serves as a kind of ethnographic primer for readers who are unfamiliar with Black Elk's cultural context.

Residents of the Pine Ridge Reservation variously refer to themselves as Sioux, Siouxs, Indian, and Lakota. Other, maybe somewhat faddish phrases such as "natural peoples," "Native American," "original people," and so forth are usually employed by nonresidents. Different persons simply use different terms. However, "Lakota," "Sioux," and "Indian" are the names most commonly used.

Books on the subject have noted that "Sioux" was actually the shortened form of an Ottawa word "Nadowessiwag" (spelled different ways within the literature), which meant "little serpents" (Baraga 1973:264). The Iroquois apparently loomed as a larger threat to Ottawa existence and so were called "Nadowe," or "big serpents." This people's regard for the Iroquois did not linger, linguistically at least, as did the well-known, surviving expletive "Sioux"— the name that adhered, over time, to Black Elk's people.[1]

Whatever its origin, "Sioux" eventually became the colloquial English word used when Lakota referred to themselves. Only in recent times have the "Sioux" begun to eschew associations with this foreign name bequeathed by their Woodland neighbors and reinforced by popular usage. Researchers have followed their lead and now employ the term "Lakota" when referring to these people.

In ages past, they referred to themselves as *oyate ikce ankantu* (literally "people native superior"), and diverse groups that composed the nation "considered one another kin" *(taku kiciyapi),* while regarding others as "inferior" *(ihukuya)* (Walker 1982:3). At first glance, such designations seem to imply a heightened degree of ethnocentrism. Monographs that take this linguistic approach, however, have neglected to show that something more is operative within the terminology.

The fuller meaning of *oyate ikce ankantu* relates also to one of the origin stories, according to which the people emerged from a lower world, with their appearance on earth implying an ascendance on top of, or above, the "inferior" realms below *(ankantu* also means "above"). This mythical underpinning of Lakota identity has been probably overlooked because of the recurrent displays of ego, or bravado, that so often characterized their behavior (Hassrick 1964:32). The earliest visitors to Lakota territory, and those who followed, never failed to mention the Sioux as being exceedingly proud (Catlin 1844; Chittendon and Richardson 1905;

DeVoto 1953; Parkman 1950). More important, perceiving themselves as "above" people was a reminder to all (variously internalized) of their cosmic identity—of whence they came and what destiny was assured, at the behest of the Sacred. It is this mind-set, or worldview, that will be seen as pivotal in the life of Black Elk. It allowed him and others to maintain a transcendent perspective on life.

Regarded as snakes or enemies by their opponents, as Sioux or Sous by Europeans, and as kin by themselves, this geographically widespread group defined its membership, generically, as being allies or friends. Herein lies another aspect of nomenclature that needs attention. Namely, three principal divisions existed among this people that, taken together, constituted the group as a whole. They did, however, maintain their own unique identities, while a loosely felt alliance existed between the divisions.

Although anthropologists have for years lumped the people under the label "Dakota," this word technically applies only to the most eastern group. Hence, those closer to their Woodland origin were Dakota, while slightly further west were the Nakota. Finally, the largest and more well-known division was the high Plains Lakota, Black Elk's people. The group to which one belonged could be detected (among other ways) by listening for the respective *l, n,* or *d* sounds in speech (e.g., *kola, kona, koda* = "friend").[2] Furthermore, the divisions *(otonwepi)* comprised subgroups (indicated below), which came to be known as the seven council fires *(oceti sakowin),* although the historical reality of this latter designation is subject to debate (Little Thunder n.d.).[3]

The Seven "Council Fires"

Dakota	Nakota	Lakota
Wahpekute	Ihanktonwan	Teton
Mdewakantonwan	Ihanktonwanna	
Wahpetonwan		
Sistonwan		

Just as the nation was thus divided into seven groups, so were the Lakota-Tetons. Like the nation, these Teton groups (called *ospaye*) were each assigned a specific place within the camp circle *(ho-coka)*.

In terms of felt identity, a given individual experienced belonging at the most immediate level. This identity did not negate, however, a more expansive self-definition. A person such as Black Elk, for example, might order his sense of belonging in at least five successively larger circles (Walker 1917:97–98):

1. *ti-ognaka*   household
2. *wico-tipi*   camp
3. *ti-ospaye*   band
4. *ospaye*   division
5. *otonwe*   blood-related tribal division

Today, these Plains folk are understood to be a geographically widespread, linguistically differentiated, nomadic and semisedentary people whose organizing principle was the camp circle. The group as a whole was conceived thus, as were the Teton of the west. Moreover, within this division was Black Elk's subgroup, the Oglala, who also comprised seven segments. The eastern divisions, with whom the Lakota had sporadic contact, were similarly arranged. Hence, daily life was carried on within a local camp, and the social configuration of this grouping eventually expanded outward to include all of the *oyate ikce ankantu*.

As central as the notion of camp circle was to Lakota life, its composition has been difficult for observers to pin down. "The encampments are not always defined in descriptions of Dakota [*sic*] social organization because they were not permanent the year round and were constantly shifting in band membership. . . . The encampments are also confused in historical literature with the smaller bands and sometimes with the larger subtribes" (MacGregor 1946:

52–53). Since this observation was made, however, the social universe of Black Elk has been studied in greater detail (due in large part to the interest generated by Black Elk himself).

Semisedentary villages were not uncommon to the eastern Dakota (earthlodges were maintained in some instances), but their presence among the Teton was unknown (Eggan 1966:45–77). Lakota camps did not remain in one spot year-round and did not always keep a fixed membership. Fluidity of composition was due to both internecine struggles and climate. In warmer weather, groups tended to come together; in winter, the large groups disbanded into smaller parties. This pattern of aggregation and dispersal reflected, appropriately enough, the exact seasonal behavior of the buffalo, the people's primary subsistence resource.

The buffalo was indeed significant, as the following extended listing of the uses of its various parts in Lakota culture clearly demonstrates.[4]

Beard: ornamentation.

Bladder: pouches, medicine bags

Blood: soup, pudding, paint

Bones: fleshing tools, pipes, knives, arrow points, shovels, splints, sleds, war clubs, scrapers, quirts, awls, paintbrushes, game dice, tableware, toys, jewelry

Brain: food, hide preparation

Buckskin: cradles, moccasins, winter robes, bedding, shirts, belts, vessels, leggins, dresses, bags, quivers, tepee covers, tepee liners, bridles, backrests, sweatlodge covers, dolls, mittens, tapestries

Chips: fuel, diaper powder

Fat: tallow, soap, hair grease, cosmetic aids

Gall: yellow paints

Hair: ropes, hairpieces, halters, bracelets, medicine balls, moccasin lining, doll stuffing, pillows, pad fillers, headdresses

Hind leg skin: preshaped moccasins

Hoofs, feet, dewclaws: glue, rattles, spoons

Horns: arrow points, fire carriers, spoons, headdresses, cups
and ladles, toys, powder horns, signals, medications

Liver: tanning agents

Meat: immediate use, sausages, caches, jerky (dehydrated),
pemmican (processed)

Muscles: glue preparation, bows, thread, arrow ties, cinches

Paunch liner: meat wrappings, buckets, collapsible cups,
basins, canteens

Rawhide: containers, shields, buckets, moccasin soles,
drums, splints, mortars, ropes, sheaths, saddles, blankets,
stirrups, bull boats, masks, lariats, straps, caps,
snowshoes

Scrotum: rattles and containers

Skull: Sun Dance, medicine prayers

Stomach liner and contents: medicines, paints, water containers, cooking

Tail, teeth, tongue: whips, switches, brushes, ornaments,
combs, choice meat

Tendons: sewing thread, bowstrings

Because of the nature of Teton camps, which alternated between fission and fusion, early observers found it difficult to understand their structure fully. Diligent research, though, has provided a fairly good understanding of how camps functioned, knowledge of which has benefited both the academic community and heritage-minded Lakota. Black Elk's generation derived their identity from, and themselves defined, the lifeblood of camp tradition, which eventually led to the contemporary reservation settlement pattern.[5]

In terms of leadership, the popular notion that Indian leaders were "chiefs" and their followers "braves" represents colloquial convenience at the expense of a more sophisticated grasp of Lakota terminology. It is true that, in recent times, the English word "chief" has often been used by Tetons themselves when referring to leadership roles, but this contemporary usage is not entirely consonant with the tradition. Black Elk himself was accorded this title, posthumously, by "some people in Rapid City," who provided his grave with a special headstone that read "Chief Black Elk."[6] Yet, the prereservation period was not so gratuitous in the bestowal of such honors. The public forum required more formal structuring.

Lakota lifeways were perhaps attributable, in large measure, to earlier events within prehistory that link the people with the equally famous Iroquois. This "league" of tribes seemed intent upon subduing their neighbors (Morgan 1962), the belligerence fanned by a felt, religious imperative, namely, that of bringing all people into one fold (the league's) as prescribed by the prophet Deganawidah (Hunt 1967; Wallace 1969). However, Iroquois militancy might have been motivated more by mercantilism than it was by a mercenary, spiritual fervor. That is, the league found itself caught within the French and English confrontation in North America, which forced woodland groups to cast their lot with whoever offered the most profitable incentives. At stake for France and England were fertile lands and a lucrative fur trade. At stake for the Iroquois was survival.

This struggle affected Black Elk's ancestors, a people whose shrouded origins seem to have been in the woodlands east of the Missouri River (Lehmer 1977:25–43).[7] Whether Iroquois aggression was due to religion, revelry, disposition, dispossession, economics, self-preservation, or a combination of all these, their sorties against the Chippewa and other groups of the Great Lakes region prompted population movements westward. What eventually became known as High Plains tribes were the descendants of folk who were probably socialized in an entirely different terrain.

Since all of this history entailed many actors in a production that took over two centuries to unfold, and since none of this drama bore the scrutiny of eyewitnesses who could in turn recount every deed found wanting or proven worthy, reasonable conjecture must ultimately be relied upon when proposing how people and events came to be the way they are (Oliver 1962). Hence, the Lakota are seen as one of many groups who converged within the Plains ecosystem, having been pushed from ancestral lands encroached upon by well-armed whites and adversarial Indians (Newcomb 1950). The aftershock of this displacement was somewhat mitigated by finding a bountiful region that provided new opportunities, but the beacons that guided adaptation were more the vagaries of experience than the wisdom of tradition. The historic period brought constantly shifting circumstances, which forced each generation "to create their own patterns of behavior" (Barrett 1984:96). Black Elk was not spared this experience. It was to serve him especially well in later, more harrowing years.

Demographic convulsions of the frontier era created for Plains groups a kind of utilitarian behavioral mode whereby expedience vied equally with convention. As a result, people like the Lakota cannot be regarded as persons inextricably bound to age-old lifeways that, if displaced, guaranteed cultural collapse. Challenges were indeed massive, but the people were accustomed to a longstanding struggle to survive.

Aided in their migration by the growing ubiquity of horses and guns, these people fanned onto the Plains like the buffalo upon which they subsisted. In fact, their adaptation was so complete that Clark Wissler concluded Plains culture to be "timeless"—extending back into the primordial past. In the case of the Oglalas, however, horses were acquired around 1750, and the Missouri crossed in about 1775. The Kiowa and Crow were extirpated from the Black Hills, which thenceforward became the sacred possession of the Lakota (Powers 1975:28).

The heart of social life that beat within the more out-
wardly observable cultural traits was everyone's sense of
relatedness to others and, ultimately, to the universe as a
whole. Ethnographies have often addressed this organic
facet of social intercourse when using such terms as "descent," "marriage," "kinship terminology," and "genealogies," but much can still be learned, as DeMallie has indicated: "A study of Lakota kin terms that strictly used
the genealogical method . . . [or] that strictly used Morgan's method of interviewing . . . would simply miss the
complexity of Lakota life" (1979:235). DeMallie further
implies that this complexity is at the heart of the Lakota
worldview itself. As a result, even though "adequate explanations of kinship, marriage, and descent" are lacking, it
is necessary to search for how the Lakota reckoned, controlled, and constructed their relatedness to one another
and their environment as a whole (Powers 1975:36). Only
after making this effort can the social sentiments internalized by people such as Black Elk be fully appreciated.

Concerning marriage, one was advised to "go to the top
of a hill and look for a wife on the other side." This wisdom
was bolstered by the aphorism, "Do not choose a wife from
the corner of your household" (Powers 1975:35). Members
of the camp *(wico-tipi)* and band *(tiyospaye)* regarded one
another as kin *(otakuye)*. Hence, dutiful youth sought eli-
gible mates outside their own band so as to avoid incest
(wogluze). Moreover, emerging youth would be told stories
that reinforced the social pattern by illustrating how marriage regulated by hormones led to one's demise. As Lévi-
Strauss noted, oral narratives confirmed "the pre-eminence
of the social over the natural, the collective over the individual, [and] organization over the arbitrary" (1969:45).

Elopements occurred from time to time, and individual
preferences in choosing a mate were acknowledged. However, a young man ordinarily courted both the girl and her
family. Ultimately, then, Lakota marriage was an exoga-

mous union that cemented an alliance between two *tiyo-spayes*.[8]

When Black Elk was growing up, the conventional court-ship consisted of males vying for the privilege of standing under a blanket with the desired, closely chaperoned maiden. (Virtuous women were prized, and so attracted more suitors.) Charms would be worn, flutes played, and gifts exchanged in a scenario that allowed the girl and her family to decide who the best choice would be. Eventually, the maiden's brothers negotiated a price for their sister that, once agreed upon, was ratified by a feast. The price involved goods such as horses and robes, and perhaps included taking up initial residence with the bride's family. The feast was called *winyan he cinakakupi,* or "he wanted that girl, so they gave her to him"—an understatement if there ever was one, given the social and economic dimensions of this very ritualized courting process (Hassrick 1964:114–18).

Marriages produced genealogies, but the fictive component of Lakota social relations was just as important, perhaps even more so. When DeMallie observed that "Lakota kinship cannot be understood [solely] . . . in terms of the traditional categories of descent and marriage," he was, in fact, calling attention to the variegated ways this people "familialized" their universe (1979:222). One could be "made a relative" through a ceremony known as *hunkapi,* a rite that conferred family status upon the initiate, who was subsequently treated as being a father, brother, sister, and so on. (Brown 1953:101–15; Walker 1982:5–6). Similarly, relationship terminology was applied to offices within social groups and to those for whom one had "feeling" or those whose behavior merited it. Terms were also bestowed on nature (earth, sun, moon, etc.), and the Great Spirit (Wakan Tanka) was itself addressed as Grandfather (Tunkashila).

Like other peoples, the Lakota considered it dreadful to

be without relatives, even though the possibility of such a nightmare was quite remote. In some form or another, familial connectedness was an operative feature wherever one looked. Whether as a visionary ideal, perceived reality, or calming assurance, the phrase *mitak oyassin* (usually translated "all my relations" or "all are relatives") was employed throughout life in the course of ritual gatherings. Year-round and lifelong religious ceremonies were a kind of perpetual goading of everyone to actualize relatedness (Sandoz 1961).[9]

Dovetailing with the above were associations one made en route to gaining status and prestige within local and larger communities. This was accomplished by gaining membership in what the literature refers to as sodalities, warrior societies, or simply societies. The Lakota word for these groups was *okolakiciyapi,* and a good number of them remained vital throughout the historic period (Wissler 1912). A variety of shaman organizations also existed (i.e., different rituals with practitioners for each), along with women's guilds or groups, (whose focus was generally religious or handicraft specialization).

These sodalities were not strictly age-graded, and a person could belong to several of them at the same time. At about the age of seven, one was invited to join a group, with full membership coming later. Officers were elected and served for specific periods of time. Meanwhile, camaraderie was the trademark of these organizations, and sentiments were fostered that blossomed into terminological designations like "brother," "cousin," "uncle," and so forth.[10] Such persons were role models who, as war and pestilence whittled away the population, became few in number as time passed. It will later be shown that the early missionaries capitalized on this social construct and established comparable organizations that today are still in place (see chapter 4).

Despite Wissler's argument that Plains culture was timeless, other observers noted contrarily that adaptation might well have been the key characteristic of peoples who forged a new life out of earlier, prairie patterns (Mooney 1907:361; Kardiner 1945:47). As mentioned before, part of this over- all strategy was an egalitarianism that, among the Lakota, certainly prevailed. Authority roles could in fact be more titular than real. Parkman observed long ago that, should the chief "fail in gaining their favor, they will desert him at any moment; for the usages of his people have provided no sanctions by which he may enforce his authority" (1950: 115-16). Whether in noncoercive leadership, rugged indi- vidualism, or social groupings that nurtured a militant esprit de corps, Plains living for the Lakota fostered social mechanisms and elicited behavior that seemed best suited for survival in an ever-difficult environment.

Leadership had to be innovative under these conditions, and standards from the past were not always suitable. In all probability, they were found wanting at times. Militancy, if only for purposes of protection, was a sine qua non of every group who competed for survival in this new locale, and this context needs to be underscored, since the popular opinion exists that these peoples were inherently bellicose. Their *new* relationship to a *new* environment required *new* ways to make relatives out of aliens. Hence, there was an expansive quality within Lakota kinship that was itself a mode of adaptation that historic documentation has fixed but that was in fact still forming or evolving for this non- static Plains culture.

Much of the preceding has focused on the more apparent traits of Lakota social organization. Although such an over- view is necessary for fully understanding how daily life was orchestrated for the culture's participants, it is equally necessary to keep in mind the religious sentiments that were ritualized and nourished on a daily basis within the Lakota universe. For the sake of brevity, it need only be mentioned that throughout the historical period virtually

every observer of, or participant in, Lakota life cited the
people's reflexive reliance on what Western scholarship
would classify as "religious observance."[11]

Whether their adversaries were human or animal, their
opponents alive or inanimate, the Lakota struggle for a safe
niche was sustained by a resilience that made them spirited
foes. This resilience enabled groups to negotiate the successful exodus west, permitted individuals to sacrifice
themselves for the common good, and was an intangible
armament within their arsenal of subsistence. It had un-
bounded limits and was rooted in the belief that all Lakota
had access to, and could acquire, supernatural power and
purpose. Before, during, and after the vision quest, seeking this power and purpose remained of paramount importance in one's life. For many, if not most, it seemed the only
constant within the changing internal and external envi-
ronments that accompanied people into the reservation
period.

The Lakota thought their continued survival was as con-
tingent upon a relationship with the Sacred as it was upon
the forces they faced in everyday profane life. This essential feature of the Lakota worldview becomes transparent
only after a careful scrutiny of persons such as Black Elk,
whose generation strove to pass on this legacy. The unqual-
ified assumption exists that religion was one of the major
cultural "traits" among a myriad that were extracted from
the Lakota world in the contact situation. The contention
here is that, on the contrary, religion was part and parcel of
adaptation for many. Black Elk's life will spell out how
such a religious identity was the underlying attribute that
remained fixed for an otherwise nomadic people of the
Plains.

▼

chapter two

▼

Genealogy

The nineteenth-century Lakota world sketched by Neihardt was foreign to Lucy's experience of family life, and thus she alluded to it only fragmentarily. This pattern surfaces throughout her account, and its first appearance is in the text that follows. In it, we are lifted into the last century and are matter-of-factly introduced to Black Elk's family as it existed when Plains culture was at its zenith. Ironically, those were years of warfare, which, in varying degrees, was a leitmotif of Plains existence from the beginning.

As her father had done with Neihardt, so does Lucy refer to Black Elk's father. Dying in 1889, he was placed on a scaffold, which was a customary burial procedure. Included within her family's genealogy was Crazy Horse (Tasunke Witko). Among many Indian people today, he is regarded as a heroic figure, whose name represents resistance to white oppression (although his representation on a U.S. thirteen-cent stamp issued on January 15, 1982, was for the less provocative purpose of acknowledging Native leadership). Killed at Fort Robinson, Nebraska, in 1877, his body was secretly disposed of by family members, and many persons have searched for his remains since that time, hopeful of recovering some tangible keepsake of the free spirit that so defied captivity (Sandoz 1942).

In Lucy's narrative, other members of the Black Elk family are likewise given attention. Neihardt may have judged them extraneous to the movement of his story, but such persons would not be so excluded by Lakota narrators. One's personal identity, for good or for bad, was largely fashioned by the individuals who composed the familial community (*tiyospaye*). Its distinct members fostered one another's values, attitudes, and existential perspective. Such is why Lucy acknowledged the different people who were part of life's daily routine within her father's world, and the world of her own home life (Medicine 1969).[1] Here Lucy recounts her family background:

My father had five sisters and one brother, but I knew just two of my aunts. My grandfather was wounded in the leg at the battle of the one hundred slain soldiers and was crippled, so my father was the man of the house.[2] He was the one who had to get out and hunt.

My father's brother died a long time ago, and I never knew him. When I was old enough to understand, I'd see my father praying and crying on a hill. He used to do that. My grandma told me, "He's crying for his brother." His name was Wicegna Inyanka or Runs in the Center. Somebody named him that when he went on the warpath.

My one aunt, Jenny Shot Close, died when I was maybe three or four years old. She was sickly and had tuberculosis, but she was really nice. She used to comb my hair. My other aunt was Grace Pretty Bird, and she is buried beside my grandma. She was a nice, quiet woman who had two children—a boy and a girl. I remember playing with my cousin, and she used to treat me mean. She'd hold me by the arm and swing me till I got dizzy. Then my grandma would really get mad. My cousins both died of tuberculosis while they were young.

I don't know where my grandfather is buried because they always used to travel a lot in the old days, and he died back then. So they made a scaffold for him somewhere.

My father always said that Crazy Horse was his second cousin, and he's dead too. My father's mother was named Mary Leggins Down, and she died in 1915. I don't know why Neihardt called her White Cow Sees. I never heard that name before. It wasn't my grandma.

During his life, my father married two times. The first marriage was a common-law marriage to a woman named Katie War Bonnet, who died in 1901. She had three boys: William, who died in infancy around the year 1895; John, who died of tuberculosis at the age of 12 in 1909; and Ben, who passed away in February of 1973.

My father's second marriage was to my mother, whose name at birth was Between Lodge but was later changed to Anna Brings White. She was a widow who was left with two children from her first marriage (to a man named Waterman). These children were Agatha and Mary, and my father adopted Mary when he married my mother in 1905. Agatha was too old to be adopted. But my sisters both died of tuberculosis in 1910.

From the marriage of my father and mother, three children were born. I was the oldest, and only girl—born in Manderson, South Dakota, June 6, 1907. My brother Henry died in 1910 while still an infant. But my brother Nicholas grew up and married, but he had the accident—that tragic accident. He burned to death in 1959 while sleeping in a small shack over in Nebraska.

I guess that since my brother Ben is now gone, it's up to me to relate a little history because I'm the only one now surviving of Black Elk's children—the same Black Elk people have read about in the books Black Elk Speaks *and* The Sacred Pipe.

Both in *Black Elk Speaks* and *The Sixth Grandfather,* "White Cow Sees" is given as Black Elk's mother's name, without explanation. DeMallie, however, has showed that there existed alternative renderings for people's names.[3] Lucy's reference to Leggins Down was said as offhandedly as one might say "Jones" or "Smith." Baptismal records note that Mary Leggins Down was born in 1844.

Given the nonverbatim mode in which Black Elk's words were recorded (DeMallie 1984b:32), it is possible that Neihardt chose a name that simply sounded exotic or mysterious (at least more exotic and mysterious than "Leggins Down"). Or perhaps Ben Black Elk, who replaced Emil Afraid of Hawk as translator, substituted this name instead of his grandmother's real one. Maybe it was simply an older name that Lucy had never heard spoken. Whatever the case, Lucy was not pleased that her brother had served in the capacity of translator, as she felt he took liberties with what her father intended to say.

Why *Black Elk Speaks* took the form it did is an interesting study in itself. According to DeMallie,

Black Elk told Neihardt very little about his later life . . . as a missionary. . . . Neihardt was curious about why Black Elk had put aside his old religion. According to Hilda, Black Elk merely replied, "My children had to live in this world." . . . For Neihardt, the beauty of Black Elk's vision made the formalism of Christian religion seem all the more stultifying, and he seems to have accepted Black Elk's pragmatic explanation at face value. (1984b:47)

Contrary to the above is Brown's opinion that revealing Black Elk's Christian participation was somehow seen as compromising the holy man's Indianness. That is, Neihardt avoided the issue and simply focused on the premodern era, highlighting "the end of the trail" and "vanishing American" themes. Similarly, "Black Elk's pragmatic explanation," taken at face value, may well have prompted Neihardt not to probe any further. However, hindsight now shows that Black Elk's full life story would ultimately be more intriguing. In taking the pulse of the holy man's true sentiments, the pages to come will show that "the formalism of Christian religion" was not an issue.

After all, Lakota religion (like others) also had much formalism, and varying preferences in the matter of religion (as in leisure, sports, etc.) may account for why some people embrace one form and some another. That is, what is life-giving for one may simply be stultifying for another.[4] Later it will be shown that "the beauty of Black Elk's vision" (subjective as such a description might be) lies beyond the stenographic notes of Neihardt's daughter, or the poet's depiction of it in the chapter of a now-famous book. These and related issues that bore upon Black Elk's life will become more transparent through the recollections of those who knew him best.

In the comments that follow, Lucy refers to an "addition" her father gave Neihardt. Since no such document exists within the poet's papers, her reference has remained elusive. Whatever the addition was, it appears to conflict with the pragmatic resignation implied by his statement that "my children had to live in this world."[5] She said:

My father related to John Neihardt an addition to his book, but they never put it out. Afterward, he realized this and wanted the last part of his life also told—his life as a Christian man praying. My father wanted it known that after he quit his medicine practice, he became a catechist. But this man [Lucy pointed to a picture of John Neihardt] really believed in the Indian religion. . . .

I shall try with all my ability to relate this untold history of my father, and I have felt guilty at times not doing this as a memorial for him. When my brother Ben was alive, we always wondered if we should do something like this. We got this idea after my father's death, and I have waited for an opportunity to relate the entire story of his life as a holy man.

My name is Lucy Looks Twice now, but I was Lucy Black Elk before I was married. And I am the only living child of Nick Black Elk. Many people have already read about my father's life as a medicine man in Black Elk Speaks *and* The Sacred Pipe. *So, I'd like to tell about the rest of his life— the many years not talked about in either book. The greater part of his life was spent as a Catholic catechist whom I knew as a meek and loving father. This is the story I know about and want to relate. This needs to be done while I am alive. My father would have wanted me to do this.*

DeMallie's efforts in *The Sixth Grandfather* certainly illumined much of Black Elk's life that previously had not been told. Besides providing a verbatim account of the Neihardt documents, the work also addressed issues that came to bear on Black Elk during his catechist years and as a result of his involvement with the poet laureate. Consequently, what follows is a kind of necessary reprise from the holy man's family and friends, who witnessed, and participated in, the events and concerns that composed this special person's life. The chapters here thus constitute an important companion volume that completes, as it were, a trilogy of portraits.

This is the final reckoning of a man who, because of his literary legacy, will remain forever the clearest voice from an Indian America that predated the modern era. Perhaps because his boyhood memories recaptured a time that seems less complex than succeeding periods, perhaps because the world he described was ecologically more pristine than what was to follow, and perhaps because his words encouraged us "to emphasize the best that dwells within us," Black Elk retains a privileged place within the constellation of luminaries whose light has been transcultural (Deloria 1979:xiv).

His decades-long appeal, however, has been based on relatively scant biographical detail. As a result, his image may
be so firmly entrenched that this portrait might at first seem
disappointing to those who imagined him to be someone
other than he was. Nonetheless, Lucy and friends of Black
Elk desired very much that this fuller story be told and that
his sacred vision be fleshed out in its totality. Far from
intending to be iconoclastic, these intimates of the holy
man sought to provide a better understanding of Black Elk
himself and of the times within which he lived. In their
opinion, his image would become even more appreciated
than it already was.

Encounters with Lucy and other contributors often included words or references that, for non-Lakota, need definition or clarification. Whereas chapter 1 addressed some
of the terms defining Lakota culture as a whole, these pages
consider certain terms that figure prominently in discussions about Lakota religion. Contemporary medicine's emphasis on holistic health might well have taken its cue from
this Plains people (Vogel 1970).

Just as the word "doctor" is collectively applied to such
divergent roles as dentist and heart surgeon, so too is the
term "medicine man" (from the French le médecin, "doctor") when colloquially referring to specialists found within
Lakota society. Today, however, "practitioner" or "medicine person" now appears in the literature, since there also
were—and are—women healers. In reality, a particular person's gifted power would be sought for addressing specific
ailments or needs.

Among the Oglala today, the "medicine man" (pejuta
wicasa) is also commonly regarded as a "holy man" (wicasa
wakan), although the two roles traditionally have been separate (Brown 1953:45n; Walker 1917:152; Walker 1980:91–
92). That is, the former referred to healers who used herbs
or applied certain skills for curing. The latter term implied
one's acquisition of mystical power, which was either put

to work on behalf of a patient or was the reason why such a person could preside at certain ceremonial occasions. Time and practice have obscured precise usage of the terms by Lakota speakers and others. Yet, in spite of this change, Lucy's narrative rightly characterizes her father as a *pejuta wicasa* before his work as a catechist. (The same phrase applied to osteopathic and allopathic physicians of the non-Lakota world.)[6] Current parlance would accord her father the title of *wicasa wakan* once he became a catechist, a phrase likewise designating the priests with whom he worked.

Having dreamed of lightning, the Lakota were obliged to undertake the *heyoka* (clown) practice, lest they be struck down by lightning. The term itself refers to the "Dakota god . . . represented as a little old man with a cocked hat on his head, a bow and arrows in his hands and a quiver on his back. In winter he goes naked, and in the summer he wraps his buffalo robe around himself" (Buechel 1970:174). As the definition suggests, behavior of the *heyoka* was profoundly nonconformist, and humor depended upon one's ability to act contrary to all norms (Thomas Lewis 1970:7– 17; 1981:100–104; Starkloff 1974:74).

At first glance, *heyoka* participation within the Lakota religious system might seem to be a peculiar mixture of secular and sacred conceptions. Such a commingling, however, has been (and still is) present within the larger, so-called world religions. Its obvious manifestation is the ubiquitous Trickster figure (Radin 1956). According to Hyers (1969:7), the rationale for so curious a phenomenon is that:

The comic spirit is fundamentally a certain attitude toward and perspective upon life. The essential element in relation to the sacred is the periodic suspension of seriousness and sacrality . . . and the realization of the playful, gamelike quality inherent in all human enterprises, however holy.

Comedy in fact plays with both the categories of reason

and irrationality, of order and chaos, of meaning and mean-
inglessness at the heart of reality itself.

In specifically addressing the *heyoka* cult within Lakota
religious tradition, Black Elk lends support to the Hyers
contention. "You have noticed that the truth comes into this
world with two faces. One is sad with suffering, and the
other laughs; but it is the same face, laughing and weeping.
When people are already in despair, maybe the laughing
face is better for them; and when they feel too good and are
too sure of being safe, maybe the weeping face is better for
them to see" (*BES*, 159–60). The *heyoka* provides the har-
monizing element to a human existence charged with emotional and psychological extremes and so keeps in check
one's tendency to distort reality. A kind of native therapist,
the *heyoka* helped people keep things in perspective (Brown
1979:58).

Whether coincidental or the result of instruction, Black
Elk's reflections on laughing and weeping curiously parallel those of Ignatius Loyola, founder of the Jesuit order (to
which Black Elk's priest-friends belonged). Referred to as
states of "consolation" or "desolation," periods of calm
and chaos were addressed at length by the sixteenth-cen-
tury mystic (Puhl 1963:141–50). Jesuits since the time of
Ignatius have been schooled in this spirituality, and they in
turn frequently teach it to others. Hence, the traditional
Jesuit understanding of this duality either fashioned Black
Elk's thinking on the subject or simply dovetailed compati-
bly with an older, Lakota approach (or perhaps both).

The following commentaries include references to the
heyoka practice and to that of *yuwipi*, the traditional ceremony associated with Black Elk in his precatechist days.
Yuwipi refers literally to "transparent stones" used in ceremonies conducted by modern-day Lakota shamans, although the word has also been rendered "to wrap around"
(Buechel 1970:656; Powers 1982:6). Its precise etymology

is unclear today. Whatever its origin, the ceremony itself, which is performed in total darkness, consists of a specialist, bound firmly within a "star quilt," who calls upon diverse spirits, which often appear as glimmering flashes. Throughout the meeting area, animal sounds and human voices are heard, having been summoned by the practitioner. Future happenings might be foretold, missing persons located, or diagnosis and cure of a given person's illness might be offered. On rare occasion, however, nonbenevolent purposes, or *hmunga* (to cause sickness), might also be the thrust of particular *yuwipi* gatherings. At the conclusion of the ceremony, the adept is seen freed of fetters, with the release being attributed to the action of spirit helpers.

Many Oglalas today regard the *yuwipi* man as representative of the old-time religion, vestiges of which are present in the ceremony. Oral history and research, however, point to non-Lakota origins of this "shamanic cult institution" (Bogoras 1904:164; Densmore 1970:44; Powers 1982; Wallace 1966). Nonetheless, "Yuwipi and Yuwipi-like rituals continue a tradition whose roots lie in the nebulous past" (Powers 1982:8). Practitioners today might be called by the umbrella term "medicine man," or by the more precise "Yuwipi."

Lucy's understanding of her father's early involvement with these older traditions is as follows:

Before being converted into the church, and before he became a catechist, my father was a medicine man. I wasn't born at that time, and he didn't talk about it very much. I remember he told us that he and his partner, Kills Enemy, were heyokas, or clowns. This clowning was actually done by him and his friend as a trial stage for them. To live the life of a heyoka for one year was a promise they had to fulfill. If they succeed in one year, then I believe they could become medicine men.

John Neihardt called Kills Enemy "One Side" in that book, but he really wasn't called that until he was an old man. *He got that name because he used to wear a hat all the time, and it always sat crooked on his head. Before that, he was always Kills Enemy to us.* [7]

He didn't talk about his medicine practice very much. However, he did say "I was kind of good at it." I almost believed him sometimes. Once I asked him, "Father, do you believe in this yuwipi?" And he said "No! That's all nonsense—just like the magicians you have in the white people. It's just like that. Praying with the pipe is more of a main thing. If a man prays with the pipe, why, people would kind of pray along with him. But this other one, yuwipi, it's just like a magician trying to fool. I know because I've done it myself."

One of my father's medicines could be found by standing out on a hill in the darkest night. He used it for curing tuberculosis. When there's no moon, you can see it. That medicine just glows. The yuwipi man uses this same medicine in his ceremony.

Once he was fooling around with his friend I mentioned earlier, Kills Enemy, and they were going to shoot an owl that was above their camp. That owl was just bothering them during the night, so they got a fire going and started loading up. They filled cartridges themselves at that time.

Just then, they were so close that a man said, "You guys! Don't get close to that fire. It's going to explode for sure!" Just then, when he said that, one of the sparks hit the powder, and everything shot up in his face. So that's where he almost lost his sight, and he's been partially blind ever since.

I got that information from Joe Kills Enemy. He was old enough to hear when his father and my father visited and talked about what they did in their early lives. He's way older than I.

I always thought he got his blindness while he was a heyoka with Kills Enemy. What I thought was that my father suggested they put a loaded shell in the ground, smash it, and see how far it goes down in the ground. Instead, it exploded up in his face. [8] *He did a lot of things like that.*

In his early years, my father had been a warrior. He was in the Custer fight, and he was in this massacre [Lucy pointed down the road toward Wounded Knee]. My father said that when all those soldiers got killed at Little Big Horn, he and a bunch of boys his age would go around and pick pockets of the dead. He said some of them found money, but they didn't know what it was.

About Wounded Knee he always said, "I was there to witness after it was over. I saw all those women and children and old people. The soldiers shot at them with their guns, and they all just laid there in the big draw. Something awful! They had no weapons—and those children massacred like that." My father carried wounded persons— women and children—over the hill to safety. They claim he said, "Today is a good day to die!" But he never actually said that. It was Crazy Horse who hollered those words. My father was young then, so he wasn't the one.

Black Elk's comment on the *yuwipi* practice is not shared by all Lakota people. As in any profession, motivation for one's involvement differed among individuals.[9] Contemporary practitioners have a sincere following, however, and their regard for the tradition is high. Persons such as Lucy might locate the *yuwipi* practitioner's special medicine and use it for other purposes, but it is still regarded as the substance out of which "spirits" take their form.

Black Elk's actual blinding is another biographical point that might never be fully ascertained. Aside from the two accounts mentioned above, another exists that tells of Black Elk's divining for water. Having placed gunpowder beneath a hole filled with water, Black Elk announced he would make water issue forth from the ground. Touching a spark to the fuse, he remained too close to the eruption, and his face was peppered with water, dirt, and gunpowder. This version was volunteered by a Manderson resident who questioned the reliability of the other accounts.

Regarding the war cry "today is a good day to die," most presume the now-popular statement refers to patriotic sentiment. That is, warriors should always be willing to die while proudly defending their families and home territory. Indeed, such was probably at the heart of the phrase when skirmishing the cavalry. An unsolicited interpretation offered by an Ottawa woman, however, carried a different meaning. "We Indians have an expression 'today is a good day to die.' It means that we should be ready to die on any given day. We should always be prepared to die, and have no regrets. That's why it's important to begin each day fresh, and not let past problems or present distractions cloud how God wants us to live." (Note that the speaker restricted this expression to "we Indians.")

Her comment is illuminating in that it shows how Black Elk material has been used by other native groups to the extent that even a war cry would be a source of reflection.[10] Whereas militants utter the phrase almost threateningly, the Ottawa woman gave a more religious interpretation. Who knows how the cult-film hero "Billy Jack" intended the phrase to be understood? At one point, the lead character solemnly announced that "today is as good as any to die!"—the Black Elk material once again authoritatively quoted, albeit erroneously, to sanction what Hollywood purveyed as authentic Indian ideology.

With the preceding traditions emerging from the material on her father's life, Lucy suggested that a visit be arranged with an old friend of Black Elk's who was still living. Mr. John Lone Goose could recall those earlier times and could provide additional commentary that was reliable.

▼

chapter three

▼

Conversion

The journey from Pine Ridge to Rushville is a little over twenty miles, and the drive is a scenic one through rolling Nebraska hills that undulate with dark, green, conifer splashes. Along the winding highway, mule deer frequently fall prey to startled automobiles. Billboards, restaurants, and residential areas suddenly appear, and within the new vista lies Parkview Nursing Home—a small facility appended to the town hospital.

John Lone Goose had been paralyzed from the waist down (the result of a car accident seven years earlier) and, because of his great size, needed the attention that only an institution such as a nursing home could provide. Apart from the paralysis, his health was excellent. He accepted his condition with serenity and said that prayer enabled him to carry on without being bitter.[1]

John's immediate family was all deceased, and more distant relatives seldom visited. Residents of the home were predominantly non-Indian, and his beloved reservation was far away. A wise elder who spoke softly and with openness,

John commanded a reverence or admiration that was easy to bestow. It was apparent that he was quite prepared to pass on.

During the course of an obligatory cigarette (a modern ritual of friendship probably rooted in the older tradition of sharing a pipe), John recounted the following indignity he suffered when placed first in a Hay Springs, Nebraska, nursing home: "I had braids that long [pointing to his waist]. They cut them. I don't know why they do it. Want me to cut my hair—that's why they do it. But I never asked what they did with my hair. The long braids! Those long braids. It wasn't quite like mine now. They were all black—coal black. But I don't know what they did with it." John's former appearance did not come as a surprise because Lucy had already spoken of him, and because one of the Jesuits referred to him in an unpublished manuscript from the 1930s as "the Giant Indian with long hair!" (Sialm n.d.:86).

Whereas braid-wearing today is common and generally reflects the trend in cultural resurgence, John was from a time when braids were still part of the living tradition. He was literally the last of a kind who could speak from the summit of many years. His was an authoritative perspective because of a long-standing familiarity with persons, places, and events.

After a short while, he came around to talking about times past, and his opening remarks include reference to the Rosebud Reservation—a large territory allocated to the Brule division of Lakota (Hyde 1961; Grobsmith 1981). Smaller in size than Pine Ridge (its western neighbor), Rosebud was the site of activity that closely paralleled Oglala history (Hyde 1937). In fact, relatives of any given family might be spread throughout the two reservations. Jesuits, government personnel, and Lakota regularly commuted between the two regions (and still do).

Spotted Tail, a famous Brule leader, requested Jesuit presence on the Rosebud, and in 1886 the order established

the St. Francis Mission. Since that time, it has served as a
school and religious center much like Pine Ridge's Holy
Rosary Mission, which was founded in 1888 at the request
of Red Cloud (Olson 1965).[2] One of the Rosebud's early,
well-known personalities was Father Digmann, who baptized John. Born in 1846 in Eichsfeld, Germany, Digmann
came to the United States as a priest in 1880. At the in-
sightful request of his superiors, Father Digmann organized diary notes into a readable commentary on his life as
a missionary among the Lakota from 1886 until 1930 (he
died in 1931). Available to researchers through Marquette
University's Archives of Catholic Indian Missions, this unpublished document contains sketches of early reservation
life that are incredibly graphic.[3] Future research on Lakota
experience of the decades around the turn of the century
should hereafter take into account this priest's unique contribution, now that it is accessible.

John provided a page never entered in Digmann's diary.
Perhaps it was not worth including from the Jesuit's perspective, as it was just part of an ordinary routine. For John,
however, the event meant everything. His parents told him
about it, but John spoke of the incident as if he were a
credible witness of the proceedings.

*On April 17, 1888, my father and mother went to Sunday
Mass in the morning at St. Francis Mission. I was in my
mother's womb at the time. While the Father was saying
Mass, and while they were sitting there waiting to get their
Holy Communion, my mother fell sick and said: "I'm going
to go out for a little while. I'm going to be right back." So
she went outside the church, spread her shawl, and sat
down. Right there—outside the Catholic chapel at St. Francis—I was born.*

*Since my mother didn't come back into the church, my
father came out to see where she was. He found me and my
mother laying there, so he went to tell the Mother Superior*

about it. Pretty soon, all the Sisters came out and took me up in the Sister's room, washed me, cut my cord, and dressed me up. They washed my mother too. At about eleven o'clock I was baptized by Father Digmann. I was the youngest one in the family—and there were fourteen of us. Now, I'm the last one still living. All my aunts and uncles, all my brothers and sisters, they all died. I'm the only Lone Goose left. There are no more by that name.

Here was Lone Goose, the one-time infant, christened "John" by Father Digmann.[4] Here was the long-haired helper of Black Elk whose great size occasioned laughter-provoking memories, such as when he and Black Elk were burying a fellow Catholic. Ever so involved with the cemetery ritual, big John Lone Goose, moving backward, lost his footing and preceded the casket into its grave. His body wedged tightly in the ground, John required the assistance of many mourners to gain release. Tears were turned temporarily to laughter through the slapsticklike misfortune of their kind-hearted brother.

Here now was the aged John Lone Goose, a gentle man who did not share the fame of his celebrated colleague and who did not have much earthly existence remaining. He provided the following recollection:

I first met Nick around 1900—when I was a young boy and he was not a Catholic. I don't know what they call him in English, but in Indian they call him yuwipi man. Sam Kills Brave, he's a Catholic, lived close to him. And before Nick converted, Kills Brave would say, "Why don't you give up your yuwipi and join the Catholic church? You may think it's best, but the way I look at it, it isn't right for you to do the yuwipi." Kills Brave kept talking to him that way, and I guess Nick got those words in his mind. He said that after Kills Brave spoke to him, he wanted to change.

Corroborating John's testimony, Lucy fleshed out the incident that changed her father's life. A key figure in this episode (and for some years after) was the Jesuit priest Joseph Lindebner. Born in 1845 at Mainz, Germany, he came to Pine Ridge in 1887 and worked there until his death on October 4, 1922.[5] The priest's small stature inspired Black Elk and others to call him affectionately Ate Ptecela, or "short father," (a phrase Lucy used interchangeably with the more formal Father Lindebner). Sina Sapa, or "Black-robe," was the traditional Lakota reference to Catholic priests, who most of the time wore black soutanes, or cassocks. Episcopalian clergy were called white gowns, and Presbyterians were known as short coats.

When Lucy narrated the following pivotal experience of her father's life, family members listened intently:

Sam Kills Brave, Louis Shields, and my father organized this Manderson community. Like we say, there is the White Horse community, White Bear community, Crazy Horse community, and others.[6] These men organized so they could help each other farm and carry on other business. Kills Brave was the main one, the leader or chief. That's the way it was in olden times. Kills Brave was already a Catholic, and he used to tell my father to make up his mind about his religious practice.

That's when in 1904 my father was called to doctor a little boy in Payabya—seven miles north of Holy Rosary Mission. The boy's family wanted my father to doctor their son because they heard he was pretty good at it. So, my father walked over there carrying his medicine and everything he needed for the ceremony. At that time, they walked those long trails if they didn't have a horse.

When he got there, he found the sick boy lying in a tent. So right away, he prepared to doctor him. My father took his shirt off, put tobacco offerings in the sacred place, and started pounding on his drum. He called on the spirits to heal the boy in a very strong action. Dogs were there, and they were barking. My father was really singing away, beating his drum, and using his rattle when along came one of the Blackrobes—Father Lindebner, Ate Ptecela. At that time, the priests usually traveled by team and buggy throughout the reservation. That's what Ate Ptecela was driving.

So he went into the tent and saw what my father was doing. Father Lindebner had already baptized the boy and had come to give him the last rites. Anyway, he took whatever my father had prepared on the ground and threw it all into the stove. He took the drum and rattle and threw them outside the tent. Then he took my father by the neck and said, "Satan, get out!" My father had been in the hundred-and-one show and knew a little English, so he walked out.[7] Ate Ptecela then administered the boy communion and the last rites. He also cleaned up the tent and prayed with the boy.

After he was through, he came out and saw my father sitting there looking downhearted and lonely—as though he lost all his powers. Next thing Father Lindebner said was, "Come on and get in the buggy with me." My father was willing to go along, so he got in and the two of them went back to Holy Rosary Mission.

Ate Ptecela told the Jesuit brothers to clean him up, give him some clothes—underwear, shirt, suit, tie, shoes—and a hat to wear. After that had been done, they fed him and gave him a bed to sleep in. My father never talked about that incident, but he felt it was Our Lord that appointed or selected him to do the work of the Blackrobes. He wasn't bitter at all.

He stayed at Holy Rosary two weeks preparing for baptism, and at the end of those two weeks he wanted to be baptized.[8] He gladly accepted the faith on December 6, 1904, which was the feast day of Saint Nicholas. So they called him Nicholas Black Elk. After he became a convert and started working for the missionaries, he put all his medicine practice away. He never took it up again.[9]

My father said that what he was doing before he met Ate Ptecela was the work of the Great Spirit, but that he suffered alot doing it. As a matter of fact, he had ulcers and had to be treated for them shortly after he started his missionary work. The Jesuits sent him to a hospital in Omaha, and he was on a diet for two or three months until the ulcers cleared up. When he converted, knowing about Christ was very important to him, and receiving communion was what he really held sacred.

People who used to be treated by him when he was a medicine man started coming to him. They asked him about the new religion he belonged to, and he explained to them what it meant. Many followed his example, and he instructed them in the new faith.

The scene sketched by Lucy was discomforting, as it seemed consistent with the oftentimes trite depiction of ill-mannered missionary versus innocent native. Taken at its face value, Black Elk's story ratified books, movies, and popular opinion that so often portray missionaries as close-minded zealots bent on destroying Native culture (Terrel 1979), and as having little of what today would be called compassion, cultural sensitivity, or ecumenism. Far from being something positive, Black Elk's experience seemed more of a deathblow to his true spirit.[10]

Lucy insisted, however, that her father did not resist Lindebner's intrusion upon the ceremony and was not angry or enraged. He did not harbor resentment and did not give in to despair. She regarded his conversion story as rather amusing and understood the event to be a great occurrence in her father's life. Moreover, she had difficulty understanding why her *takoja* did not join with the others present, who laughed and smiled in hearing of the incident. Here was an amazing story and humorous tale being told (she thought), but he had remained expressionless while listening!

Apparently, the factors most important to Black Elk on

this occasion were these: (1) a holy man was present, (2) the holy man's powers were known to be very strong, (3) resistance to such power was unthinkable, (4) Black Elk regarded his power as negligible by comparison, and (5) he was predisposed to changing his religious practice. That the priest was of another culture, that he was a white man, and that he was seemingly so indiscreet, pushy, or insensitive were not important. What mattered was Wakan Tanka, whose action was apparent and could not be challenged. Such was, at least, the tentative interpretation for a story that captivated two distinct listening audiences for two widely differing reasons.

According to Lucy, her father had "suffered a lot" while practicing as a medicine man and had experienced quite a bit of inner turmoil. This experience, along with Kills Brave's entreaty and a persistent stomach disorder, reinforced Black Elk's desire to seek some kind of relief. He knew that something was not right in his life, and the symptoms were, minimally, social, physical, and psychological. After his visit to the hospital, during which time he received the Catholic sacrament of the sick, Black Elk undertook the work of a catechist, and his ulcers were never again bothersome. Lucy said that her father felt "the son of God had called him to lead a new life." The Christian Lord known as Wanikiye had "selected him" to do this work.

In the opinion of several Manderson residents who heard Lucy's account of the story, liberties were taken in telling what probably transpired. Although no one claimed to speak with certitude, it was commonly assumed that medicine men such as Black Elk would not allow themselves to be pushed around in that fashion. Similarly, the priest had a reputation for being very kind and gentle and could hardly have been the ruffian portrayed.[11] All agreed, however, that something out of the ordinary occurred in Black Elk's life, although the exact details were quite difficult to pin down.[12]

Digmann and Lindebner knew one another well, and their work on both reservations was similar in scope. Allowing for idiosyncratic differences, Digmann's experiences and reflections may have paralleled those of Ate Ptecela. He wrote the following about his first encounter with a Lakota medicine man:

A pagan Indian . . . called for a priest to baptize his dying child. I went with him on horseback to his camp, about three miles from the Mission. One of our school girls, already baptized, had dressed the one-year-old boy nicely and put a small crucifix on his breast. He was asleep. After we had said the Our Father, the Apostle's Creed, I baptized the child "Inigo." For a couple of days he had taken no nourishment, as the mother had no milk.

A boy went with me to the Mission to get milk and medicine. Mother Kostka, who was a good nurse and had knowledge of medicines, wished first to see and examine the sick child. We went on foot under the parching heat of the sun to the Indian camp, the white veil of the Sister was soaked with perspiration. A short distance before the log cottage, Grace Anayela met us saying: "The medicine man is conjuring the sick child, I do not want to be present." Arriving at the door, we heard their singing, beating the drum. . . . What a spectacle! In a corner of the room, the father was sitting with the naked child in his arms. Along the wall four conjurors were crouching, with their faces painted red and yellow. One of them had returned from an Eastern school, understood English fairly well and spoke it tolerably. Him I addressed first: "George, you here?" He had asked me already before to baptize him. Then I continued in Sioux the best I could at the time, "Give up your devil's work. The child is baptized and belongs to the Great Spirit." George said: "Do you want that one of us shall die?" "You will not die, get out of here." They, however, continued their pow-wow, singing and ringing pumpkin shells. On my repeated

*begging they finally kept quiet. Mother Kostka examined
the little patient and wanted to make hot poultices.*

*The conjurors had spread out on the dirt floor of the
loghouse their medicine bags. There were also bowls with
water, and a pan with burning coals. To gain room, I removed . . . the deerskin bags, gave the water to the Sister,
and put the coals in the stove to start a fire. Horrified they
looked at me, thinking perhaps that the Evil One would
hurt me. George flung the satchel of the Sister out of the
open door. The scared mother took the sick baby outside,
the Sister followed. George, angry, grasped my arm to put
me out, but I stood the ground. In the presence of them I told
the father of the child, not to allow them to continue their
conjuration, and not to let their leader take the child to his
house. They promised. The firmness seemed to make an
impression. George became cool. He said he did not believe
himself in this pow-wow but there was money in it. They
make the parents pay in ponies, blankets, or other valu-
ables, while at the Mission and at the Agency they would
get medicine gratis. (MACIM:8–9)*

A similar situation is reported for April 6, 1909, wherein
Father Lindebner himself is mentioned. Digmann wrote:

*Osmund Iron Tail called me out of Catechism class saying:
"Jim Low Cedar would die today." He was going to the
agency to get a coffin. James was a boy of ten years, had
been at the Mission over two years, but owing to a slow fever
was allowed to go home. We told his mother, who had been
baptized not long ago: "Call the physician and give his
medicines. If you know of any good Indian medicine, you
may also give it, but do not allow any conjuration, sacred
songs, etc. of the medicine man." Iron Tail told me that she
had first done so, but seeing that the Whiteman's medicine
did not improve him, she had called for an Indian Medicine
Man. Now, Father Lindebner had visited the sick boy and*

administered to him Extreme Unction but could not give him yet the Holy Viaticum. When then the medicine man came making arrangements for his pow-wow, Little Jim peremptorily refused it saying: "The Little Father [Lindebner] has anointed me; I don't want to be conjured, I want to go to heaven." When Iron Tail reported this, I said within myself: "Jim, you deserve also Holy Communion." Arriving there, I found him fully conscious and glad to receive the Blessed Sacrament. After a short preparation and prayers, he received his Lord for the first and last time with visible devotion. Three hours later he took his flight, to see Him in heaven.

It is not surprising that Lindebner encountered Black Elk under the circumstances he did. According to Digmann, "The sickbed is the field, where the physician (medicine man) and priest (missionary) often meet. We had a special eye on the sick, not to let them go without baptism. Several of these died soon after baptism, and the opinion was spread by the medicine men that pouring on of water had killed them"(8).

Such scenarios were commonplace, it seems, as the Lindebner obituary illustrates.

On one occasion, he broke through the ice while crossing Little White River, and one of his horses was drowned. Father Lindebner himself was almost frozen to death, yet the same night he borrowed another horse and made his way to a dying Indian. Only three or four years ago, when over seventy years of age, he made a sick-call trip of four hundred and twenty miles in the face of a keen blizzard that brought the thermometer well below zero . . . three years ago, the writer was returning from a trip with the holy old priest, when on nearing the mission we were informed of a dying man some miles back on the road. We returned forthwith to the Indian's cabin and found the patient lying on blankets and pillows on the ground outside his house. After Father Lindebner had done what he could for the poor fellow, the latter begged us to sing some Indian hymns for his consolation and encouragement . . . for an hour we sang all the hymns we knew and some, I fear, we didn't know. The result was more noisy than harmonious. But it seemed to please the sick man. (IS1923:84–86)[13]

Lucy was not familiar with the Digmann material. Rather, she simply reported the tale told by her father. Perhaps Lindebner was indeed too gentle a soul to match the conversion story's persona, and perhaps Black Elk would not have tolerated anyone's intrusion upon his religious ceremony. Perhaps the type of experience Digmann reported in his diary was well known, and maybe Black Elk's otherwise undramatic conversion story drew more listeners when garnished with details from somewhere else. Maybe the type of interaction Lucy reported frequently occurred, however, and simply did not elicit controversy at all (as it does for those removed from the times and places).

Black Elk's story might belong to a special genre, namely, an oral narrative telling a biographical truth via incidents that never actually happened quite as reported. Lucy, for example, could relate the story and, with her family, appreciate its import. Unfamiliar with this form of communication, a non-Lakota could listen to the story with disbelief or chagrin and consequently miss the point intended.

Lucy told of her father's conversion on several occasions, and she never failed to mention that "dogs were there, and they were barking." Her words appear to be straightforward in their description of events, but more seems to be at work than Black Elk (or Lucy after him) simply recounting a play-by-play account of what occurred. The inclusion of barking dogs is a significant embellishment that would lend additional force to the story among Lakota listeners. As William and Marla Powers have written:

Dogs are considered useful for protecting the house from the incursions of strangers, as well as for announcing the presence of friends. Anyone living on the reservation soon becomes accustomed to dogs barking all night long, and the reason for their nocturnal howling is frequently discussed the next morning, because dogs herald not only the presence of humans but that of ghosts as well. In Lakota . . . the expression sungwapa, "dog barking," is a metaphor for any general commotion. (1986:7)

By saying that dogs were barking, Black Elk (or Lucy) perhaps used a type of literary formula that established a frame of reference for the conversion event. Spirits were present, and they signaled that something important, extraordinary, or mysterious was unfolding. The dramatic effect of this narrative element would be lost on a non-Lakota audience. It thus is probable that the tale falls within a traditional genre, one that authenticates the experience itself.

Religion particularly might lend itself to this narrative form, as Christianity has an analogous story within its Scripture. Judaism's Saul was en route to Damascus to persecute Christians when all of a sudden he was knocked to the ground and blinded (through, it is assumed, divine intervention), leading him to change his name (to Paul) and religious practice (to Christianity). Christian fundamentalists might interpret Paul's experience literally and assume that he had in fact been knocked down and then blinded, physical events that ultimately led to his conversion. Other Christians, however, might look beyond the extraordinary details of the account and simply conclude that Paul was somehow profoundly changed or converted on this occasion. Lucy even mentioned that her father's experience was like Paul's.

Black Elk's own presentation of the drama of Payabya, whether whole or partial in its statement of concrete fact, unambiguously signaled for him the decisive call from

Wakan Tanka through a Wanikiye Blackrobe. Such was the basic import of the holy man's experience, and his life after this event constitutes the most solid testimony to such an understanding. Such an understanding can embellish or delete whatever it was that actually represented the life-changing occurrence near a dying child in 1904.

Paul Steinmetz said of Black Elk's conversion story that the experience resulted in an "integration of the two religious traditions on a deep emotional and even unconscious level" (1980:158–59). DeMallie asserted otherwise. He noted that Black Elk's conversion was "unquestionably genuine" but that the acceptance of Catholicism placed him "beyond the onerous obligations of his vision" (1984b:59,14). As this study progresses, a more curious and complex series of experiences will be shown to unfold within the holy man's life that beg a more expansive interpretation than those proposed thus far.

An initial building block of reinterpretation can be excavated from the classic ethnography of religious experience by psychologist William James (1961). His work was one of the first to address conversion as a phenomenon to study instead of an experience simply to take for granted or dismiss as psychological instability. His observations are apropos of Black Elk's life: "To be converted, to be regenerated, to receive grace, to experience religion, to gain assurance, are so many phrases which denote the process, gradual or sudden, by which a self hitherto divided, and consciously wrong, inferior and unhappy becomes unified and consciously right, superior and happy, in consequence of its firmer hold upon religious realities" (James 1961:160). As was the case with Black Elk, "religious aims form the habitual centre" of one's energy after such an experience (165). As a result, it is not surprising that questions surface in regard to the facts of Black Elk's conversion story. According to James, "Neither an outside observer nor the Subject who undergoes the process can explain fully how particular experiences are able to change one's centre of energy so decisively" (165).

A more contemporary evaluation of this process can also help explain what was at work in Black Elk's life. Proudfoot has said that it is not the subject matter of religious experience that is as important as the explanation of it given by the individual (1985:231). Being ineffable, such experiences beg articulation through symbol or metaphor, through poem or story, or through whatever mode that one can utilize as a vehicle for expression. Black Elk's conversion narrative seems to have been a product of this very personal, and very profound, experience.

▼

chapter four

▼

Catechist

The overview of Lakota culture in chapter 1 indicated that men and women highly valued their participation and membership in warrior, curing, dancing, hunting, handicraft, and other special-interest groups. In the postreservation period, however, these sodalities began to disappear (Lowie 1948:294). As they did, Lakota Catholics were organized into two religious organizations known as the St. Joseph and the St. Mary societies, and these groups were received quite favorably. They assumed a prominence formerly reserved by the traditional associations.

Louis J. Goll, S.J., onetime director of the Jesuit community at Holy Rosary Mission, related this history of the *okolakiciyapi* (societies) of St. Mary and St. Joseph:

The Benedictine Fathers working among the Sioux . . . organized two societies, one for men, under the patronage of St. Joseph, the other for women, under the protection of the Mother of God, and called them the St. Joseph and St. Mary Societies.

St. Joseph, the other for women, under the protection of The Jesuit Fathers introduced these societies in their missions. Accordingly, the Catholic Brules and Oglalas would meet every Sunday, whether or not a priest had come to them for services. One man, elected and approved for that purpose, led in a kind of lay-service: hymns were sung, and specified prayers were recited. This finished, the president ("grandfather") gave a well-thought-out address on an article of the Creed, on the sacraments, or on the Commandments of God. This done, he would appoint two or four men as speakers on the same subject. Such was the meeting of the St. Joseph Society.

The St. Mary Society also had its program. The president ("grandmother") would address all present. She, too, would appoint two or four speakers, there being excellent speakers among these Indian women, able enough to drive home a lesson for men and women alike. Then the grandmother would give a resumé and hand back the presidency to the grandfather. (1940: 36)

Throughout the year, meetings were held and were well attended. Besides gathering for prayer and song, members would discuss religious issues and plan parish activities. After the first fifty years, membership in the societies declined, and the core participants became the now-elderly children who had been born in the early reservation period. The ebb and flow of religious involvement in recent times, however, has made the fluctuation unpredictable. Other institutional expressions have also arisen—most notably, in Catholic circles, the Tekakwitha Conference, a national organization named after the Mohawk maiden whose piety was reported in *Jesuit Relations* (Kenton 1954:293–95).

The major annual event planned by the societies was the Catholic Sioux Congress. This three-day gathering of Catholic Sioux from all the reservations first started in 1891 at the Standing Rock Reservation, on the border of North and

South Dakota, and has occurred every year since then at different locations selected by the membership.

Usually held around the Fourth of July, this religious convention was instituted by the missionaries for several reasons. In earlier times, many Lakota would gather yearly and celebrate their unity against the backdrop of the Sun Dance. Building on this older religious tradition, which was outlawed in 1881, missionaries organized the summer congress as an opportunity for new church members to see and support one another in their faith (Goll 1940:39–43). Moreover, it was felt that an event so specifically tailored to Native interests would be a more suitable celebration for a people to whom Independence Day had little or no meaning. Generally, the agent would distribute thirty head of cattle to the tribe for purposes of celebrating the national holiday. When congresses first started, the Catholic population requested that these cattle be given to the societies!

Before automobiles were in much use, caravans of wagons could be seen taking society members and their families to the assigned rendezvous, with each family carrying its own camping equipment. Shortly after arriving, as many tents as wagons dotted the hills of the congress site—Oglalas from Pine Ridge in one section, Brules from Rosebud in another, and so on.

Three days of praying, singing, receiving sacraments, exhorting, and friendly visiting would ensue. Well over three thousand Lakota participated in this event fifty years ago, although attendance has steadily decreased. As recently as thirty years ago, nearly a thousand representatives were present, but this number dropped to a couple hundred just a decade later. Even so, those who still attend the event have an eager anticipation long months before it occurs.[1]

Society members have lamented the dwindling number of congress participants, and their concern has been evident since the 1940s. In that Lucy's generation represents the mainstay of the societies, younger members stress the need to update the event's proceedings and focus more religious activities around Lakota youths. However, such reforms as the speaking of English rather than the traditional Lakota, or initiating a youth congress, have repeatedly been voted down.

Black Elk's involvement with this unique institution was considerable. Being a catechist, his duties included organizational details, preaching, and instructing new converts. This ever-active participation in society work and congresses molded Lucy's religious formation. Tenets cultivated by her father were absorbed during early childhood, as the following recollections show:

We'd go along with him to the congress and the Catholic general meetings, and all the catechists would show up. On all kinds of Catholic holidays—Easter, Decoration Day, Christmas, New Year's—the catechists would get together at their parish chapels and have services. And on these occasions I often heard my father instruct the people about Scripture.

He related Scripture passages to things around him, and he used examples from nature—making comparison of things in the Bible with flowers, animals, and even trees. And when he talked to us about things in creation, he brought up stories in the Bible. That's why he was a pretty strong Catholic—by reading the Bible.

On one occasion, my father and the old faithful catechist Fills the Pipe were attending a meeting and were camped side by side. Fills the Pipe had a crippled wife, who could hardly do anything. So one night, my father was coming back to his camp when he heard someone hollering.

A lady was hollering, so my father went down to see what happened. Anyway, this Fills the Pipe had been hauling water from the creek, and he fell just as he came up with the buckets full of water. Again, he slipped and fell.

The third time, his lady just couldn't take it, so she sat down and started hollering. That's when my father went down to help this poor old man carry his water. That's the way these catechists ran into hardships with their families.

Building upon what the culture already had in place, the societies established leadership roles and communal activities for the Catholic population. Their success also was enhanced by a Catholic clergy who "held a somewhat more tolerant attitude toward Indian ritual and custom" and who, "being celibate, were more mobile" than their Protestant counterparts (Marty 1970:9–10). Furthermore, religious nomenclature (i.e., Father, Sister, Brother) employed by the Catholics also sounded a positive note for Native listeners, whose social universe was glued together by kinship.[2]

Where Native deacons and priests today serve as clergy among the people, catechists were the lifeblood for the societies (and the Catholic population as a whole) in times past. According to Duratschek (1947:206–7), these men were:

selected for their intelligence, good character, and zeal, [and] were the agents who carried out whatever the missionaries proposed. They met periodically with the priest who instructed them in what they were to teach those natives whom the missionary would not reach the next week or two. On the Sundays when Mass was not offered in their districts, the catechists led the prayers and hymns of the gathering, be it in a tepee, log house, or chapel. After reading the Epistle and Gospel for the day, they instructed the people. When necessity arose, it was the catechists who baptized and who buried the dead. They visited the sick and informed the priest when anyone was in danger of death.

More was involved with this type of religious commitment, as Lucy's memories of her father show a man who took this responsibility so seriously that for many years it was a way of life the family as a whole accepted as their own. But Black Elk was not an exception, or was not alone, in pursuing this course within the new order of twentieth-century Plains life, as the recollections that follow indicate. Lucy recalled:

I don't know why they did this, but even the Episcopals chose the medicine men—like my father's uncle over here. You'll probably hear about him later on. Black Fox they call him.[3] He was a medicine man—a great one. And here he got converted to the Episcopal church, became a preacher, and even became a deacon before he died.

A good number of the early catechists were medicine men—like Paul and Joe Thin Elk. But they quit and turned back to the old ways. One of them told my father: "Brother, I am turning back to the old medicine." And my father answered: "That's up to you." As I said earlier, after my father was baptized, he promised to do away with his early practices. Since he was a catechist, he lived up to it. He never gave up his prayer or what he was taught.[4]

At the time, we had a three-room log house with one room for my grandma, who died in 1915. My father raised horses and pigs, while my mother had chickens and a milk cow.[5] They plowed up the ground and grew potatoes, corn, beans, and other vegetables. My mother helped him with this, and we seemed to have enough food, because my father built a cellar in which they kept most of it. Although he drew only ten dollars a month for his missionary work, it seems we never went hungry.

Right after his conversion, he went back and was supposed to take care of the Manderson district. He gathered all his friends, called a meeting, and then asked his friends and relatives to help him build a place—a little house in which to have Mass when the father comes. Somebody donated a horse to them, a work horse, which they traded for logs. They then built the first St. Agnes Church and meetinghouse. It wasn't too big, but at least they had something ready for the priest. And so that's where my father started—right from that little log house. He was the first catechist of St. Agnes Chapel. They appointed leaders and had a big Christmas party—giving presents to all the older people, the real old ladies and real old men. They called them by names and gave them presents individually.

After the Jesuits baptized several in each district, they pretty soon began to get men like my father to be catechists. In every station they appointed two or three catechists to work with them. These laymen were trained to conduct services, read Scripture on Sundays, baptize if necessary, visit the sick, and bury the dead. But most of all, they were trained to teach the Catholic faith.

There were catechists in all those little communities like Grass Creek, Rocky Ford, White River, and Pine Creek. I know Alec Two Two was the catechist in Wounded Knee, which at that time was called Brennan, South Dakota. William Cedar Face and Kills Enemy were the catechists in Grass Creek, while Frank Gallego was down in Rocky Ford. Silas Fills the Pipe took charge of the community out there at Red Shirt Table, while Joe Horn Cloud took over at Potato Creek. John Fool Head was at Slim Buttes. Many others were also catechists at the time of my father, like Red Willow, Jim Grass, Louis Mousseaux, Daniel Broken Leg, Willie Red Hair—and Ivan Star Comes Out was at Our Lady of Good Counsel on the other side of Oglala on the White River. Men were catechists from all the different districts. And when it came along that my father was called away to other reservations for missionary work, Paul Catches took his place.

Since my father was one of the first catechists, the Blackrobes might come for him at any time to go on a trip. So right away he had to work—and he worked. They used to come for him very often, and he was really willing to accept

any kind of trip they were supposed to make—even in the
coldest weather. He would go with Father Lindebner or
Westropp or Father Henry Alder, and people would come to
them, attend Mass, and even have their young ones bap-
tized. There would be converts, and he would teach them.

The Catholic church in Manderson today is still named
St. Agnes. Unlike its cabin predecessor, it now is a larger,
white, wooden structure looking like a typical country
church. The meeting hall behind was dedicated to Black
Elk's memory. However, the sign that commemorated this,
which reported his tenure there as a catechist, was torn
off the building not long after the 1973 occupation of
Wounded Knee—according to popular suspicion, by members of the American Indian Movement (AIM).

Black Elk's friend Paul Catches was the father of Pete,
who also became a catechist. Now a practicing medicine
man (Zimmerly 1969:46), Pete is no longer formally involved with church work, even though his ties with Jesuits
are still strong. The ceremony he conducts is not *yuwipi* (as
some local people charge) but rather that of *wanbli* (eagle),
performed largely for healing purposes.

Pete's ceremonies (or sings, *lowanpi,* as such occasions
are also called) are easy to confuse with those of *yuwipi*
(Feraca 1962). In the darkness of a small cabin, with participants sitting cross-legged on the floor, he orchestrates
an entrancing, prayerful, sensory experience that includes
singing sounds and faces touched with light brushes of
eagle feathers and water droplets. He does not, however,
get tied up (as reported for the *yuwipi* ceremony earlier).
Persons present utter prayers of thanksgiving (or need) in a
room so pitch-black that the atmosphere is one of disem-
bodied voices. Pete has often been the guest of priests and
other interested parties at meetings that address differences and similarities of Lakota and Christian religious tradition (Stolzman 1974, 1986).

Catechists at the Catholic Sioux Indian Congress, 1911, at Holy Rosary Mission. Black Elk is sixth from left, wearing moccasins.

Another highly respected reservation elder was Ben Marrowbone, a man whose ties with the past were far more intimate than those of most residents. He was from the generation of Lakota patriarchs whose parents were the last to experience nomadic Plains life. During his active years, Ben worked as a catechist, undertaking this labor when Black Elk was still an active missionary himself.

Lucy thought Ben perhaps could add to her own narrative, since he was known to be very devout in his religious practice and was considered a "true traditional" within the reservation community. He was one of the leaders pressing Lakota claims that the Black Hills be returned to the people. Mixing Lakota with English, he used hand gestures to lend power to what his words communicated. He was just as willing to discuss those days long past as he was of speaking to government officials about the Black Hills (maybe hoping both would be, somehow, returned before his death). According to Ben Marrowbone:

I drove the team, and we used to start from here [Holy Rosary Mission is across the road from Ben's cabin]. We'd go

Catechists attending the Catholic Sioux Indian Congress of
July 1920. Black Elk is in bottom row, far left.

to Slim Buttes, Wanblee, Sand Hills, Eagle Nest, and every
district. It took three or four weeks sometimes. I was tired
when we came home.

There'd be no meetinghouse or no church, so we'd bring
bedrolls. Brother used to bake a big loaf of bread for us,
and we'd take a box of chicken, some potatoes, and sauerkraut too.[6] We went to every house in a district, and
we stopped before sundown. We would talk to each other.
"You want to stay there overnight?" "Sure!" You see, different people would want us to come in. Some people had a
bedstead, but sometimes the father and I would sleep on the
floor. We'd spread our bedrolls and sleep together.

One time we went to bed about eight o'clock. It was a
cool night, and we had a bedstead to sleep in. Father Lindebner nudged me as we fell asleep and said: "We aren't
alone. Little animals are sleeping with us." That bed was
filled with little bugs.

In the morning, strong coffee would already be cooked—
and we'd have to drink it. And grease bread, we'd eat it
too. Father then offered Mass at that house and people

nearby would come. They'd explain their confession, their sins before God. Remember, everybody makes mistakes, so we tell Almighty, and he forgives them. The people understood this, and they truly believed it.

John Lone Goose adds:

That book, Black Elk Speaks, just talks about the olden way. But I remember every detail of what he did because I was with him—not every day—but every time the father would come over, or when he would teach somebody who wanted to be a Catholic. I was there to help him.

The priests gave him instructions in the faith, and Nick said he wanted to teach God's word to the people. So he kept on learning, learning, learning. Pretty soon, he learned what the Bible meant, and that it was good. He said: "I want to be a catechist the rest of my life. I want it that way from here on!"

So he went around as far as Norris, Kyle, Potato Creek, Porcupine, and all those districts. He'd go around preaching with Father Buechel, Father Lindebner, Father Perrig, Father Louis, Father Henry, and all those old priests. Lots of people turned to the Catholic church through Nick's work.

He never talked about the old ways. All he talked about was the Bible and Christ. I was with him most of the time, and I remember what he taught. He taught the name of Christ to Indians who didn't know it. The old people, the young people, the mixed blood, even the white man—everybody that comes to him, he teaches—from the Bible, from the catechist book, from his heart.

He was a pretty good speaker, and I think Our Lord gave him wisdom when he became a Christian. For even though he was kind of blind, his mind was not blind. And when he retired and was sick, he still taught God's word to the people. He turned Christian and took up catechist work. And he was still on it until he died.

Left to right: John Lone Goose, Father Sialm, and Ed White Crow at Manderson, 1928. (Courtesy of the Buechel Memorial Lakota Museum.)

Lucy contributed these memories:

Sometimes he'd be in bed and somebody would come saying there was a person dying who wanted to receive the sacraments. And so, even at night he'd go and pray for them. If they were already baptized and had been receiving the sacraments, he would call for the priest in the morning. Lots of times he would have to ride to Holy Rosary Mission [thirteen miles distant] on horseback in order to get a priest to come and administer the last rites to a sick person.

During the times he was home, he'd go on sick calls or have prayer services for other families. When someone needed to be baptized, he would call the priest. Or if there was a Mass, he would serve it. On Sundays, when the priest couldn't make it for Mass at a particular chapel, the catechists were trained to read Scriptures, put on a prayer service, and make a sermon. My father did these things and learned all the prayers by heart. And in lots of cases, when the priest was not there, he administered baptism.

The people really liked to sing with my father, and Mr. John Lone Goose would play the organ—by ear. Whenever they had Mass there, he was playing for them. They right away caught on to the singing, and they really liked to do Indian hymns.

Of course, my father never had any experience in this kind of work before he was baptized, but still—right away he understood what it meant. He had poor eyesight, but he learned to read Scripture and prayer books written in the Indian language.[7]

Pretty soon, I was so interested.

As a small girl, I was trained in praying those Lakota [i.e., Catholic] prayers and Lakota Indian hymns by my mother. She taught me how to read in Indian too. She really taught me a lot in praying and singing. I wanted to receive Holy Communion, so I really tried my best. Well, my father and mother thought I was old enough at the age of seven years.

Ever since I was six years old he trained me in prayers— Indian prayers—and Indian Catholic hymns. There's one song—the first song he ever taught me was this song here. I'll sing it right now.

Wakantanka lila waste
Slolyeic iya cin ce;
Oyas tanyan iyuskin po,
Niucantepi nicila.
Lakota oniyatepi,
Koyan ekta up ye;
Jesus niyuhapi kta ce
Heon oyas nicopi.

O God most good
Who wants to make himself known,
All rejoice rightly,

He asks of you your hearts.
You Lakota are a nation,
Quickly may they come together;
Jesus would have it so,
Because he has called you all.

My father liked it. I guess that's why I like it.

They told me that I was baptized the same day I was born. I was born a Catholic the same day I was born a Christian. And my father raised me a Christian-Catholic. That's the only thing I was taught by him.

I made my confirmation in Rapid City at the Immaculate Conception Cathedral. Of all my father's children, there was Ben, my younger brother Nick Jr., and myself—he had us really trained in the Catholic church. We had to do what he asked, and we had to attend Mass every Sunday.

Today I have a great devotion to the Sacred Heart, I myself. One time my younger brother Nick had a hemorrhage. He was bleeding from the nose. He was dying. I didn't know what to do, so I knelt down. My father and mother were broken up—saddened—so I knelt down with them. We prayed the rosary and the Sacred Heart prayer.

While he was laying there, my brother said: "I want some prayers said to St. Theresa." I don't know why he said that, so I said a prayer to the Little Flower of Jesus. Afterward, when he got well, he told me he saw that Little Flower—that Theresa. He said: "I know it was her."[8]

Not all of Lucy's recollections were as dramatic as the above. In fact, Black Elk had some humorous experiences that Lucy found quite memorable. When she related the episodes that follow, the family members present took great delight in hearing them. By contrast, the day-to-day routine of her father's life at Oglala (a community to which he was assigned as catechist) is more soberly stated in Father Buechel's diary. The entry for December 23, 1928, reads:

"Mass, sermon & 12 Holy Communions at Oglala. Drove home. On the way, Black Elk & I prayed for Mrs. Charles Eagle Louse who is sick" (MACIM). Other dates, containing scant information, show Black Elk sponsoring for baptisms and present at various religious gatherings.

Lucy continues her stories:

My father was appointed catechist at Oglala, so we moved there. My father would often have services and come home by himself real late at night. My mother would leave a lamp burning near the window so my father could find our house—as it was out in the country. Anyway, one night my father came walking home, but all he saw were tall trees and bushes. My mother had forgot to light the lamp, and my father was lost.

He started shouting "hey, hey," but my mother was sound asleep and didn't hear him. I woke up right away and poked my mother saying, "Mother, there's my father shouting outside." So she got up, opened the door, and saw my father about ten feet away from the house looking the other way. You see, his sight wasn't too good at the time, and he didn't know he was so close to home. That's why he was shouting for help.⁹

On another dark night my father came home riding our big white horse Baloney. Baloney was so well broken that you could just let the reins drop and he wouldn't move—he'd just stand there. When my father came home, he got off the horse and went to open the corral we had nearby. After he opened the gate, he turned around and was really scared. A white ghost with big black eyes was right behind him—looking at him. My father real quickly punched that ghost in the nose, and was he surprised to see Baloney run off! You see, he didn't realize that Baloney had followed him to the gate and had turned to face him. That horse *didn't come back until the next day.*

Father Henry Grotegeers used to ride a motorcycle when he went around to say Mass. My father was at Holy Rosary Mission one day, and Father Henry asked if he would help assist at the services in Oglala. So my father got on the back of the motorcycle, and the two of them started off. When they got to the church, Father Henry couldn't stop the motorcycle, so he headed for the racetrack that used to be there. They went around and around that track until Father Henry decided to head back to the mission. My father held on all the time wondering why they couldn't stop.

On the way back to the mission, Father Henry changed his mind and figured he would stop that motorcycle by driving it into a bank. So he crashed into a bank on the side of the road, and he and my father were thrown off. My father shouted at Father Henry, "You nearly killed me!" But when he told us the story afterward, we all laughed and laughed.

Another time, one of the missionaries came along to get my father for a trip. So my father said: "I'm going to get my clean clothes on." He was in such a hurry that he rushed to the suitcase and started dressing. They [Lucy's mother and father] must have both used the same one, for when he put on his underwear, he was wearing those things [Lucy points to the chest area]. It was my mother's underwear he put on!

He was mad. He went to my mother and said, "Woman, put your things in a separate place from here on!"

And another time, during Christmas, he was resting. For any big feast or holiday that came along we used to stay overnight in the addition to the meetinghouse. So everybody was getting ready for the Christmas party—putting up the tree and preparing for services. When they were ready for prayer to begin, they called my father.

Right away he went and got his coat and threw it over his shoulders. All the coats were hanging on nails. So there he was leading prayer in front of all the people on that cold night—wearing my mother's coat, which had real high shoulders.

When he finally sat down, one of the men near him said, "Cousin, you've got a nice coat on. Where'd you get it?" My father then went over to my mother and said, "You hang your coat someplace else!"

My father went with Father Westropp way over to the Cheyenne agency, and they had to cross the Cheyenne River. When they got there, it was flooded, so my father said, "Father, I don't think we'll be able to cross it." But Father Westropp said, "No, Nick, God is going to help us. He'll take care of us." So they went into the water.

Well, it was so high that the horses were swimming, and they were just barely hanging on to the buggy. All their belongings just floated away—their Bibles, prayer books, bedding, and even their food. On the other side were some people who came to rescue them.

These people took Father Westropp and my father to their camp, and everybody's clothes were just all soaking wet. They clothed them, fed them, and gave them a place to sleep. They even gave them hats—cowboy hats. So that's the kind of life they had in those days.

When he was older and retired from his church work, my father did that inipi, that sweatlodge, with some other men. Georgie was outside and in charge of opening the flap when they needed air. Well, we had a windmill nearby, and Georgie went and climbed it just when they wanted that flap opened. I heard them shouting for Georgie, but he couldn't get down. Since that sweatlodge was for men only, I didn't want to open the door, and I told them Georgie couldn't get down. I wasn't going to open that door. After I said that, my father shouted right away, "Daughter! Open that flap now or we'll burn up in here!" By that time, Georgie had climbed down and could open the door—so, they *were really glad to finally get some relief. It was really hot inside.*

One time, he went and took his buggy and team to the store. As you know, he was a pretty talkative man—so while he was there, he forgot about his buggy and team. After he came out to go home with his groceries, his team and buggy were gone! They had left him and went home. After he got a ride, he found them back at our place.

Another time, he rode to the store and left his horse in the front. He then came home, but forgot that his horse was tied up on the rail.

Although Lucy regarded the above incidents as simply humorous happenings from many years ago, those related to wife and horses suggest another level of meaning at play. Several of the episodes show, in one form or another, an indirect reproof (*heyoka*-like) administered by Black Elk to two types of creature with whom he had to contend. Layers of interpretation aside, however, everyone who knew Black Elk recalled him as a man with a good sense of humor.

Even in the account of his participation at the massacre of Wounded Knee, Black Elk made a statement that reflects his *heyoka* upbringing. Finding soup in a deserted *tipi* north of Pine Ridge, he and his friend stopped and helped themselves to it. Soldiers were in hot pursuit of the two men, and bullets whistled in and about the *tipi*. After one bullet struck too close, Black Elk casually stated, "If that bullet had only killed me, then I could have died with *papa* [dried meat] in my mouth" (*BES*, 224–25). Neihardt (or Ben) may not have detected his statement as being intentionally humorous—an example of comic relief during a narrative of woe. Similarly, readers of the early Black Elk material might so solemnize his utterances as to miss this comic facet of his personality. It was preeminent, however, in the memory of those who knew him.

▼

chapter five

▼

Missionary

Black Elk was a catechist whose efforts were not restricted to the Pine Ridge Reservation. As the following recollections show, he was employed as, and enjoyed being, "a kind of a preacher" among groups other than his own. Lucy recalls:

The Jesuits also took my father to other different tribes— even though he couldn't understand their languages. He instructed Arapahos, Winnebagoes, Omahas, and others— teaching them the Catholic faith with the help of an interpreter. At that time, these tribes were going for peyote and had been influenced by their neighboring tribes. But he converted a lot of these people.[1]

Sometimes I would have to sing in front of the Catholic gatherings. I had always been with him—I and my mother, and also my younger brother—and he would say to me, "Never be ashamed to pray or sing, because if it's for God— praising him and praying to him—you'll be rewarded by his blessings in the future."

62

So I learned a lot through him—and understanding. If it wasn't for him, I don't know what I would have done. Through his teaching and training me, I stood strong in my faith. There's something about this Christian life never failing. If anything went wrong with my children, if he prayed, I knew everything would be alright. He had a way, since he said he loved little children.

Even though he ended up with a lot of sufferings and trials, he still went strong—even when two of his children died and he had two caskets in the church.[2] He stood by, still preaching because he was loved by everybody.

One thing he always hoped and prayed for in those days was that a Sioux boy would become a priest and a Sioux girl would become a nun. And I think he was rewarded because I've known a girl from our district who became a Sister. And from the reservation, there are several of them.

He sure was interested in that kind of life. Everything in the Scriptures he understood. He knew. Members of the St. Mary's Society always came to him for advice and asked him what church work they should do in the future.

One of the Jesuits with whom Black Elk had considerable interaction was Eugene Buechel. Born in Germany in 1874, Buechel first arrived among the Lakota in 1902 at St. Francis Mission. From that time until his death in 1954, he worked with the people of Rosebud and Pine Ridge as a missionary-priest-linguist and was held in very high esteem. In 1923 he published *Bible History,* and in 1939 *Grammar of Lakota.* Having taken extensive field notes during his many years on both reservations, Buechel's collection of Lakota words and definitions remains unmatched. Jesuit priests compiled his notes into a dictionary in 1970, which remains today the authoritative reference on the Lakota language.

His name is legend among older Lakota speakers, one of whom said: "We can't teach the young people how to talk Indian. The only man who ever spoke it perfect was Father Buechel, and he's dead." Another aged consultant recalled speaking to Father Buechel and not knowing the old words used by the priest. Buechel kept a diary during his many years, which contains, aside from pastoral concerns for the area, a daily statement about the weather (MACIM).[3]

On November 14, 1906, Father Buechel made the following entry in his diary: "Nick Black Elk had come to collect money at an issue in Rosebud. As it came off later, he made three days retreat. I gave [it] to him. He asked 'How is it about eating during the retreat? The Indians do not eat during their recesses.'" The incident here reveals Black Elk's attempt to understand his newer religious practice against the backdrop of his older one. Fasting was common to both traditions.

Lucy could not assign a date to an experience that her father spoke about in later years, but it occurred at St. Francis Mission and might have taken place at the time of the retreat mentioned above, or during other visits there, which continued for years.

My father was at St. Francis when they were going to have a burial of a little baby in a casket. They brought the one that died into church, so he went in and sat down to pray. That casket was there in the church overnight, and they were going to have it buried the next day.[4]

My father was in the church that night when a certain Sister kept coming to the casket. Three times she came. Finally, she asked my father to tell the rest of the mourners that she wanted the casket open so she could see the little baby that was in there. I guess they let her.

They opened the casket, and they found the baby was alive! And this Sister, my father told us, must have had a special sense for that child. Anyway it was a girl in that casket, and she grew up to be an older woman.

Before his departure in 1916 as a missionary to India, Fr. Henry Westropp, S.J., authored a pamphlet entitled *In the Land of the Wigwam: Missionary Notes from the Pine Ridge Mission* (MACIM). In this very brief, fifteen-page account of his experiences among the Lakota, he refers to Black Elk's work as a catechist in much the same fashion as did Lucy. He wrote:

Many of the younger men who are capable are given duties as catechists, and many of them are and have been faithful companions for years, gladly abandoning wife and family for weeks at a time to help the missionary in his work. One of the most fervent of these is a quondam ghost dancer and chief of the medicine men. His name is Black Elk. Ever since his conversion he has been a fervent apostle, and he has gone around like a second St. Paul, trying to convert his tribesmen to Catholicity. He has made many converts. At any time of day or night he has proved himself ready to get up and go with the missionary. On any occasion he can arise and deliver a flood of oratory. Though half blind, he has by some hook or crook learned how to read, and he knows his religion thoroughly. On one occasion a preacher asked him if he thought it right to honor the Blessed Virgin. The following dialogue took place. Black Elk asked him:
    "Are the angels good people?"
    "Yes."
    "And St. Elizabeth, is she good?"
    "Yes."
    "And the Holy Ghost?"
    "Yes."
    "Well, then, if all these honored her, why should not I?"[5]

When she was a small child, Lucy accompanied her father to other reservations where he was assigned. One was the Wind River Agency of Wyoming, home of the Shoshone and Arapaho. Here he worked out of the St. Stephens Mission, which, like the other Jesuit institutions, served as an educational facility and religious center. Another sojourn was at the Marty Mission (Duratschek 1947:273–311), a similar operation directed by Benedictine priests some two hundred miles east of Pine Ridge. Not particularly apparent in this part of the account, but poignant in its telling, was Lucy's profound admiration for her father and his work.

Staying at Marty was less challenging than at other places, and the Yankton people with whom they lived were particularly receptive to Black Elk's visitation. Both Lucy and her father enjoyed their time among the Yankton and returned often to encourage the developing faith-community. Lucy continues:

When I was three years old, my sister Mary died. She and Agatha used to go to Holy Rosary, so when we went to St. Stephens in Wyoming, I used to go around and cry trying to find her. I thought she was among those Arapaho girls.

Finally, they thought I was going to be sick, so my father spoke to the superior and said he was going to bring his family back home. Just before that, my younger brother Henry died.

Later on, my father and James Grass went back to the Arapahos, but that tribe had been quarantined against what they called "sores"—which was the German measles. They stayed around until the quarantine was lifted and wanted to get in contact with the main leaders. But most of them were on peyote, especially the Shoshones, so my father and Grass gave up on them and got ready to leave.

Then a chief of the Arapahos came into where my father was staying, grabbed him by the chest, and made the sound of a bear. Then it looked as if he wrapped something up and threw it out. The chief then said, "You're not strong or brave enough to go through with us. We were thinking about your Christianity. We were having a meeting thinking about you." That man said he would bring his people for instruction.

So my father went to get a permit from the agent. During the quarantine, they couldn't have any gatherings, and the agent still didn't want to give them permission for dances. My father got the permit for the church gathering, but he had also told the people to bring their Indian costumes to Mass so that afterward they could have a feast and dance. He knew they liked the dancing. So some of them even wore their Indian costumes to church. That was the only way they could have their dances for a while. A lot of them joined the church and got baptized—even peyote people.

That's when they first started Christmas night dancing. Everyone would go to midnight Mass, then have a feast, and then dance. They'd break up real late. After my father retired, he and Jim Grass visited them. They found out that they continued that dance—only now it was for an entire week up until New Year's. I don't know if they still do that.

When I was small, maybe five or six years old, the missionaries appointed my father and three others to go east. The places I know he went were New York, Boston, Washington, D.C., Chicago, Lincoln, and Omaha. They were trying to lecture for the Oglala Sioux who were becoming Catholics and who were in need of chapels and other things. Somebody served as interpreter for them.

After this trip, he told us about his experiences. He said, "In some towns, we'd go down the street or to some special occasion and some white people would throw rotten eggs or tomatoes at us. That happened in some places, but in others a lot of people were real good to us." I think he meant the kids were bad to them. He even visited prisons, like Sing Sing in New York. He tried to talk to them and convert them.

At one place he said he was up there talking and saying to the audience: "You white people, you came to our country. You came to this country, which was ours in the first place. We were the only inhabitants. After we listened to you, we got settled down. But you're not doing what you're supposed to do—what our religion and our Bible tells us. I know this. Christ himself preached that we love our neighbors as ourself. Do unto others as you would have others do unto you." At that early time, he said those words. He told us that when he was finished speaking, everybody clapped.

He told me about the white people he had met when he was in the East. He said they were coming like a big river through the land and that I must try and learn at least how to speak English so I could get along with them and compete with them. He didn't hold anything against them, but he always cautioned us to keep our land and work on it—like we're doing now. We have a garden and have had one every year.

When I was six years old, we went to Marty, South Dakota—where the Marty school is now located. There was a house for the catechist to stay in, and my father was the first one to use it. He went around with Father Westropp instructing and baptizing the people. On Sundays they have Mass, and my father would serve for it. He knew how to serve.

We stayed there over a year, and I used to play with the Yankton Sioux children. When I came back home, my friends all laughed at me because I talked like a Yankton. Also during this time, the little Yankton children and myself, we all learned the Latin responses for Mass. After he retired, my father used to put my kids to sleep by singing one of the Latin high Masses. It would work too. You just had to say something to him once, and he caught on.

Black Elk himself recounted his missionary experiences in a publication that circulated around this time. Apart from simply reporting what he did, the catechist would also pass on to readers his religious philosophy, as the following selection shows:

I have seen a number of different people—the ordinary people living on this earth—the Arapaho, the Shoshone, the

Omaha, the tribe living in California and Florida, the Rose-
bud, the Cheyenne River Sioux tribe, the Standing Rock,
and our own, the Oglalas. The white men living in all these
places—I have said prayers for their tribe. I'm really moved
that I was able to travel to these places and meet people that
are very friendly. . . . In all these, good things come from
God because of your faith. The United States—all the peo-
ple—should have faith in God. We all suffer on this land.
But let me tell you, God has a special place for us when our
*time has come. (*Sinasapa Wocekiye Taeyanpaha, *July 15,*
1909)

Because of his time in Europe and travel throughout the
States, Black Elk developed a worldview that included more ✓
than the Lakota Reservation experience. This background
provided him with new perspectives, religious and intel-
lectual, that later proved advantageous in his work as a
catechist. His travels gave experiential substance to what
he said.

How Black Elk's missionary journeys sometimes got
started is revealed in the following correspondence
(MACIM). In it, another style of self-expression is attributed to the holy man, quite unlike that fashioned by
Neihardt some twenty-odd years later, and by someone else
just a year later. Similarly, his work among the Shoshone is
cautiously acknowledged by a missionary who mentions
Black Elk was good, but not as effective as one of the men
who accompanied him (i.e., Grass).[6]

Writing in English through an interpreter (of questionable grammatical skills) to the director of the Catholic Indian Missions, who was stationed in Washington, D.C.,
Black Elk sent the following letter in 1908:

Dear sir. Wm H. Thatchman
if you wants have a church in your country why I wish
you let me know.

We was in saint Stephen Wyoiming. and we make have a
church. so.
   if you wants same is that. why you let me know.
   and shonshone indians they wants to me to do it same
   you remember me in prayers your friend
     Nick Black Elk, Manderson S.D.

A year later (September 7, 1909) a better interpreter
seems to have been found, as Black Elk again expressed an
eagerness to be on the road doing church work.

Rev. Father Wm H. Ketcham
Washington D.C.
My Friend
It is long since I have not written to you. About two things I
want to speak to you. The Assiniboins in Canada want the
prayer. They want to see me very much.
   The other thing is this: I want to take care that many
children in North and South Dakota join the Society for the
Preservation of the Faith.
   Therefore I want to go round for 2 or 3 months. I want to
hear what you think about that. My sister died.
With a good heart I shake hands with you
Nic. Black Elk
Address: Manderson P.O.   S. Dak.

In a 1915 letter to the Bureau of Catholic Indian Missions
now in MACIM, Father Westropp described Black Elk as a
catechist who was "doing great work," and in an exchange
of letters (one by Black Elk), the matter of catechist's sal-
ary is raised. *The Sixth Grandfather* reported that their pay
was five dollars a month (1984b:16), whereas Lucy said
her father received ten. The Bureau of Catholic Missions
"thought it was $15.00," while Westropp and Black Elk
understood it to be twenty-five dollars! Perhaps Lucy's recollection was, after all, one related to the disparity between

negotiating parties (i.e., a difference of ten dollars). Or
perhaps the wage simply changed over time. Whatever the
amount, Lucy made it clear that her family was not in need.

Marquette University's Catholic Mission Archives contains other letters exchanged between Fathers Ketcham,
Westropp, and Buechel related to Black Elk's missionary
trips and compensation for them. As director of the Bureau,
Ketcham was besieged with correspondence from missionaries and catechists nationwide, which included a flood of
reports and requisitions. In Black Elk's case, the catechist
would write of journeys to different reservations and his
efforts to promote the faith. Generally, he would ask for
Ketcham's continued support of the trips and mention the
need for some kind of travel expense.

Ketcham would then try to corroborate Black Elk's comments with the priests out in the field. Both Westropp and
Buechel affirmed the catechist's labors but cautioned the
director against subsidizing him beyond what they had already provided. Westropp's 1909 letter, referring to Black
Elk as Uncle Nick, assured Ketcham of the catechist's pros-
perity and, as in Buechel's letter of 1912, noted the frequent tendency of such men to beg. An evaluation of these
exchanges given by DeMallie is that "holding to Christian
doctrine, he practiced the virtue of charity to the fullest.
On the other hand, he was able . . . to fulfill the traditional
role of a Lakota leader, poor himself but ever generous to
his people" (1984b:23). This understanding, and not a
more critical one, seems apropos as Black Elk's reports
from Manderson, published in *Sinasapa Wocekiye Taeyanpaha,* reveal him zealously committed to the work of
catechist. That is, his toils were not self-aggrandizing. The
content of these articles reflects what Lucy described as the
gist of her father's preaching (more excerpts of which appear
later on).

Lucy often relayed information that presumed knowledge
of persons and events connected to Pine Ridge history. She

did not realize the need to explain a cultural vocabulary unique to her Lakota upbringing and probably wondered why her father's biography could not be drawn together after one session. Some of her references needed clarification, as in the case of the Ghost Dance.

 At times called the Messiah Craze, the Ghost Dance of the 1880s was a Native religious movement whose most vocal adherents were from among the many Lakota bands. Rooted in the teachings of a Nevada Paiute named Wovoka (also known as Jack Wilson), the Ghost Dance was received as the answer to a prayer. Suffering from confinement to a drought-stricken reservation, and dying from disease and starvation because of inadequate food allotments and failed crops, a good number of Lakota fervently embraced a doctrine they heard would end such misery (Mooney 1896).

 Word was received that a second coming of the Christ was close at hand. Whites had killed him years earlier, so this time he would deliver the Indian people, restore their buffalo, raise the dead, and vanquish their foes. Wovoka is reported to have preached a doctrine of nonviolence and resignation, but among the Lakota his teachings took on a militant cast that eventually produced tragic consequences (Utley 1963).

Besides gathering to dance for a return of the dead, people like Short Bull and Kicking Bear advised that a speedier end to their troubles would occur if "Ghost shirts" were worn and resistance asserted against whites.[7] The shirts were thought to have the power of deflecting bullets, and any form of submission to reservation law would only delay liberation. Consequently, a hostile atmosphere prevailed throughout Lakota country in 1890 as growing numbers looked with longing to the spring of 1891 (when deliverance was expected). Meanwhile, government injunctions against these ideas and practices seemed only to underscore their validity. The oppressors knew they were doomed, or so went the thinking, and the exhaustive, trance-producing dance became the order of the day. Father Perrig's diary reported for December 15, 1890, that "Fr. Craft has seen last night the ghost dance performed in the Rosebud Indian camp. He found it to be alright, quite Catholic, and even edifying" (MACIM). Unfortunately, this perspective was not shared by government personnel.

Sent to intercept Big Foot's band of Minneconju dancers, cavalry troops mismanaged surrender negotiations and precipitated the now-infamous massacre of Wounded Knee on December 29, 1890. After a mass burial of over two hundred men, women, and children, and with the spring of 1891 giving birth only to the summer, protective shirts and a second coming became dreams-turned-nightmare. The Ghost Dance hope was dead, even though the conditions that produced it were not. The following account can be understood better with this history in mind, since Black Elk interacted with persons who were very involved with Ghost Dance activities and knowledgeable of the Christian themes it included. In Lucy's words:

At one time, Father Lindebner said to my father: "Nick, go over there, and I'll have Mr. Fills the Pipe go along with you to instruct a very old lady so she can be baptized pretty soon. I'll come along later."

My mother said I wanted to go, so my father hooked up the team and we went down the creek below Manderson toward Rocky Ford. When we arrived there, this old lady was in a little log house shack all by herself—next to a bigger house where the people who took care of her lived.

We went in and she greeted us, and my father instructed her. Afterward, Father Lindebner came.

My father asked the old lady, "Unci" (that means Grandma), "do you want to be baptized and join the church?" Right away she said, "Yes, everybody is getting baptized, so don't leave me out." She said she was willing to answer every question they asked.

So my father said, "Do you believe in the Catholic church?" She said, "Yes." And then he said, "Do you believe in Jesus Christ, who came down from heaven?" And she said, "Yes, I know that long time ago." Right away she looked at Father Lindebner and said, "But I heard the wasicus [white men] were bad, so they killed him." We'd take that as a joke today, but they didn't. They just went on instructing her, and pretty soon she was baptized and willing to receive communion.

After that, although she was pretty old, she walked to St. Peter's Church.[8] I guess she really believed in the faith, because she used to walk slowly, but she always did get there to receive her Communion. Then she'd walk back to her shack again.

She was really rewarded with a happy death. The priest was there, and she received her last rites and communion. And that's one I witnessed myself.

Another time Father Lindebner came over to baptize my grandma and her cousins. They were all living together and were ready to be baptized because they had already been instructed. And again there was my father and his friend (he says it's his cousin) old man Fills the Pipe, who was trying to make them say the Acts of Faith, Hope, Charity, and the Act of Contrition.

He was trying his best to make them say the prayers along with him, but they were kind of blundering. Fills the Pipe would tell them: "Say after me." And one old lady would repeat, "Say after me" each time he'd begin a new sentence.

They were going so slow that I took my fancy little cup. I had it ever since I was a small girl. I took my cup, filled it with water, and went around baptizing my three grandmas. That Father Lindebner—I really like him. He just stood there looking at me pouring water on each one and said, "Hurry up with the prayers, Lucy has already baptized all the old ladies!"

I guess I really took to everything, and I'll always thank my father for training me and giving me a good Catholic life. But that's the way they were. He and my mother were really interested in church work.

In those days it was fun to get a lot of the older people baptized. Sometimes they'd understand, and sometimes they wouldn't. They might ask a woman what name she had chosen, and she might say "Jacob," or some other man's name. Or one man said, "I want to be called Julia." So, things like that happened in the old days.

Since my father and mother trained me as a helper, I had to teach the younger people. I had to go along with my father to teach them prayers in Lakota—like the Our Father and Hail Mary. And I had to tell them stories in the Bible, like when the Lord was born in Bethlehem.

Anyway that's the way I followed them around. And my father told me to do my duty as a Catholic—go to Mass, receive the sacraments, and never forget to thank Wakan Tanka for the blessings and benefits he has bestowed upon me. He always said, "To live close to God is more enjoyable than to live easy—with all the pleasures and riches—because such things never will reach to heaven. One thing is never lie, too, because you will lose all your honesty toward God and your neighbors."

When I took communion, I knew that Christ came into my heart. He was present on the altar, and he came to my parents and my heart. I used to play with my dolls and make believe they received communion. I'd dress them in white and put that little veil on them and make believe they made their first communion.

I also used to go out in the garden when I was a little girl and shake hands with the corn stalks. "Good morning," I would say to these creatures. And I would pray with them.

Another time there was going to be a Christmas Midnight Mass, so my father told me to go to bed early. He said that "tonight Jesus comes into the church"—and we all believed *exactly that (since Christianity had just been taught to the Indians). Anyway, I got up, dressed, and went into church.*

After I went out of the house, my mother must have put a doll above my bed as a present. I also had a stocking hanging there, so they filled it up with candy and nuts, and on top of it they put a big apple. When I returned from Mass, I didn't notice anything. I just went to bed. I didn't look around.

Next morning, my father sang an old song with the words: "Get up and see what you've got above you." He was singing that, and I knew he meant me. So I looked up, and here that doll was hanging there. And my stocking was filled with candy and things I really enjoyed. That was the first time I ever had a doll. Later I went to school at Holy Rosary, and Father Buechel gave me a doll too—a nice little doll that I had for a long time.

When Lucy started school, she lived at Holy Rosary Mission the better part of a year. Apart from holiday sessions, she would see her parents when they came to visit. Upon completion of her eight years of formal education, Lucy remained at home until her marriage. Efforts to secure a more detailed pattern of her father's life always met with a calm restatement of information already recorded. Namely, when not actively engaged in teaching, preaching, or other time-consuming church activities, Black Elk maintained his home and attended to responsibilities he had as the head of a family. Lucy continues her recollections.

Well, it came to pass that my father said I must attend school at the Holy Rosary Mission and that I couldn't go along with them on the missionary trips. He said, "Now since you're a girl and not a boy, I want you to take music lessons and learn all you can. So after you get out of school, you're going to be playing for the Mass and for all Catholic gatherings. That way you can serve God. If you were a boy, I would have you trained as a catechist."

*So I did. That way I thought I would please my father. Yet,
I learned afterward that the Sisters who taught me music
actually worked for the service of God, and it was actually
a heaven-sent talent that I learned from the Holy Rosary
Mission.*

*I was an organist for the last thirty-four years, and some-
times I still play when I'm in a good mood—but sometimes I
have a little rheumatism, so I hardly ever play anymore.*

*When we went to the Holy Rosary Mission, my father
and mother didn't even notice that I wore my beaded moccasins. I also wore a velvet dress that had ruffles on it, and
my hair was long. So my father brought me to school, and
my mother stayed home because she hated to see me go.*

*Father Buechel went and got a box with a big red apple
on it and said, "I got something that you'll really like." So I
looked in the box and there was a doll—the kind that slept.
My dad was there to see if I was going to cry—because my
mom told him to take me back home if I did. But I passed
him and went to the school clothing room with Sister Gen-
evieve. She took away my moccasins and gave me some
real thick shoes, black stockings, and a big heavy dress
with ruffles.*

*I was at Holy Rosary when my grandma died, and I
didn't know anything about it until my father, mother, and
baby brother came to visit me. My mother had her hair all
down, like in the morning when you get up, and it wasn't
braided. She wore black, and when she saw me she hugged
me and was crying as she said, "Your grandma died."*

When Lucy related the above incident, her words were
slowly and solemnly uttered. The loss of her grandmother
some sixty years previously seemed painfully immediate.

Black Elk, in front, with his wife, Anna, and Lucy, with her hands on boy's shoulders, after a "home mass" near Oglala in 1937. (Courtesy of Heritage Center, Red Cloud Indian School.)

▼

chapter six

▼

Life Story

Lucy could recall very little about Neihardt's visit with her father, but Father Sialm's diary reflects a viewpoint held by some within the Catholic population at the time *Black Elk Speaks* was first published in 1932. Some objected to the book not so much on what was related but rather on what was left out. Neihardt's supposed life story covered only twenty-four years of the man's life, which they felt was an injustice to Black Elk. Nothing had been mentioned about his long years of labor as a Christian missionary among his people. Excerpts from Sialm's diary illustrate this rather strongly felt position.

Concerning Black Elk's relationship with Father Sialm and other Jesuits, Lucy said: "Oh, he liked all of them, even though they said Father Sialm really got after him sometimes.[1] But he didn't mind that. Father Sialm was my confessor, but I didn't know much about him." Lucy's sentiments regarding the publication of *Black Elk Speaks* paralleled those expressed by Father Sialm, but she and the priest's successors have come to value Neihardt's work as an important contribution to Lakota heritage, however incomplete its rendering of Black Elk himself.

Placidus Sialm, born in 1872 in Disentis, Switzerland, first came to Pine Ridge in 1901. He died there in 1940. His use of the word "pagan" should be understood here and elsewhere to mean a person who has not been baptized into the Christian faith. He wrote in his diary as follows about Black Elk:

He was very zealous . . . and went much around with Fr. Westropp. He became catechist and traveled to other reservations under direction of Fr. Westropp. He was well educated in the faith.

Nic Black Elk could have finished the book with a fine chapter of his conversion. But Neihardt did not want that. . . . Nic as Catholic did more for his people than as medicine man before. Nic was in his best years when he was converted and he knew that the Gospel was clearer than his dream. Nic had many fine speeches about the Catholic faith in big assemblies, at congresses in several places. But all that did not suit Mr. Neihardt.

For quite a few years Nic Black Elk made the Catholic retreat under Fr. Sialm and what he learned then was more than all the dreams of the Indian medicine men. After one of these retreats Nic Black Elk came to Fr. Sialm with the solemn declaration: "We Indian catechists have resolved never to commit a mortal sin." It was Nic in the name of all who made up the resolution. In our great procession of Corpus Christi, Nic Black Elk was prominent in leading the real Indians in their costumes in the procession. It was perhaps the greatest exultation of his heart when he saw so many Indians following up to Corpus Christi Hill in Oglala and in Manderson in perfect order and knowing & firmly believing that the living Christ was among and with them all to bless them & their country. He saw then more horses lined up than in his dream. [See chapter seven for a discus-

sion of Black Elk's "vision," here referred to as a "dream."]
With 9 years Nic Black Elk could for a truth not count the
horses which he pretended to have seen in the dream. But
perhaps it was rather Mr. Neihardt who by all force put
things together to suit his own purpose. Black Elk cannot
read the book as it stands and cannot object against the
forceful contortion of the poet.

The greatest injustice, however, is that Black Elk is left
under the impression that now as an old man he is in despair
about fulfilling his destiny for his people. He has done wonderful good work for the truth & the way & the light which is
Christ, and His one holy catholic apostolic Church. We, as
missionaries whom Black Elk calls Fathers, are obliged to
protest against the injustices done to Black Elk—one of the
worst exploitations ever done to an honest Indian. This book:
Black Elk Speaks has no "placet" and no "imprimatur"
from Black Elk. It could fairly be put into the class of not
only exploitation, but what is worse, of stealing—plagia-
rism—material for a book, cleverly done, a kind of kidnap-
ping the very words of a man . . . and translating them into
a new language to disguise the fraud.

We missionaries have learned the language of the Indians. We lived with them not only a few months. We know
their good and bad qualities. But we feel that the Indians
have sacred rights to be respected. If a book cuts out the
very best from a man's life under his very roof: this is not to
be left unchallenged. We know that Black Elk would not
conclude his narrative as did Mr. Neihardt. His son Ben
Black Elk said that the last chapter was not in the intention
of his father.[2]

Black Elk did not divest himself from Christianity to fit a
poet in such a manner as to stand before the world as a real
old time pagan. It badly befits an old man to dissimulate.
In the old Book we read of a man in his old days who would
not dissimulate but would rather die to keep his good reputation and to be an encouragement to young people than a

stumbling block [2 Macc. 6:18–31]. Black Elk knows that story. He is man enough and Christian in addition as not to fall back from the holy command which was delivered to him by his missionaries. He knows better than Neihardt the words of Peter II, 2:22. Black Elk knows all those truths and stands for them. If it were in his power he would solemnly protest against this book, especially against the last chapter added without one consultation by the writer.

Let him speak as a pagan up to 1900—but after baptism Black Elk solemnly protests to stamp him again a pagan. In the last 30 years since we knew Black Elk this Indian stands up as a Christian, knowing & professing Christ the true Messiah and his only church with Peter, the Rock, as guide & light. It is wonderful to have a solemn Declaration of Black Elk with regard to his firm & solid Catholic faith signed by himself & declared before the whole world. This Declaration should stand in every new edition of Black Elk Speaks. The members of his parish St. Agnes Manderson & all the Catholic Indians on Pine Ridge Reservation will gladly testify that Black Elk is one of their true & sincere members & should not stand before the world now in his old age as an old time pagan and medicine man. Black Elk is a true Christian.

Such a declaration was finally made but never reached the presses as a postscript. In short, feelings were hurt, as the following document reveals.[3]

Holy Rosary Mission
Pine Ridge, S. Dak.
January 26, 1934
Black Elk Speaks Again—A Last Word
   I shake hands with my white friends. Listen, I speak some true words. A white man made a book and told what I had spoken of olden times, but the new times he left out. So I speak again, a last word.

I am now an old man. I called my priest to pray for me and to give me holy oil and the Holy Food, the "Yutapi Wakan." Now I will tell you the truth. Listen my friends.

In the last thirty years I am different from what the white man wrote about me. I am a Christian. I was baptized thirty years ago by the Black-gown priest called Little Father (Ate-ptecela). After that time all call me Nick Black Elk. Most of the Sioux Indians know me. I am now converted to the true Faith in God the Father, the Son and the Holy Ghost. I say in my own Sioux Lakota language: Ateunyanpi—Our Father who art in heaven, Hallowed be thy name—as Christ taught us to say. I say the Apostle's Creed and I believe every word of it.

I believe in seven Holy Sacraments of the Catholic Church. I myself received now six of them: Baptism, Confirmation, Penance, Holy Communion, Holy Marriage, and Extreme Unction.

I was for many years a regular companion of several missionaries going out campaigning for Christ among my people. I was nearly twenty years the helper of the priests and acted as Catechist in several camps. So I knew my Catholic Religion better than many white people.

For eight years I made the regular Retreat given by the priest for Catechists and I learned much of the faith in those days. I can give reasons for my faith. I know Whom I have believed and my faith is not vain.

My family is all baptized. All my children and grand-children belong to the Black-gown church and I am glad of that and I wish that all should stay in that holy way.

I know what St. Peter said about those who fall away from the Holy Commandments. You white friends should read 2 Peter 2:20, 22. I tell my people to stay in the right way which Christ and His church have taught us. I will never fall back from the true faith in Christ.

Thirty years ago I was a real Indian and knew a little about the Great Spirit—the Wakantanka. I was a good dancer and I danced before Queen Victoria in England. I made medicine for sick people. I was proud, perhaps I was brave, perhaps I was a good Indian; but now I am better.

St. Paul also turned better when he was converted. I now know that the prayer of the Catholic Church is better than the prayer of the Ghost-dance. Old Indians danced that kind for their own glory. They cut themselves so that the blood flowed. But Christ was nailed to the Cross for sin and he took away our sins. The old Indian prayers did not make people better. The medicine men looked for their own glory and for presents. Christ taught us to be humble and to stop sin. Indian medicine men did not stop sin. I want to be straight as the black-gown church teaches us to be straight to save my soul for heaven. This I want to do. I cheerfully shake hands with you all.

   signed: Nick Black Elk
         Lucy C. Looks Twice
         Joseph A. Zimmerman, S.J.

Concerning the above declaration, DeMallie thought its translation tended to "slant the document slightly more in Christian idioms" and so retranslated it for *The Sixth Grandfather* (1984b:61). A second document, written eight months later (appearing below), shows that a certain dissatisfaction, difficult to assess, continued to linger after the book's publication.

Joseph A. Zimmerman, a signatory to the first letter, was a Jesuit priest who figured prominently in the life of Black Elk and other Lakota over many years. He was born in 1884 in Westphalia, Wisconsin, and spent thirteen years at the St. Francis Mission before coming to Holy Rosary in 1930. Hoping that Black Elk would not be misrepresented again, he did not look favorably on an upcoming visit with Joseph Epes Brown. But where Brown would remember Zimmerman as somewhat of an impediment to fieldwork, medicine man Pete Catches considered the priest "a saint who I pray to."[4]

As to the purpose for writing not just one, but two, declarations, DeMallie suggested that some of the missionaries were disturbed by the Neihardt portrayal and did not let the matter rest. He goes on to speculate that Lucy was perhaps "the actual author of the letter" (1984b:62n). Written from Oglala on September 20, 1934, it reads:

Dear Friends:
Three years ago in 1932 a white man named John G. Neihardt came up to my place whom I have never met before and asked me to make a story book with him. I don't know whether he took out a permit from the agent or not. He promised me that if he completed and publish [sic] this book he was to pay half of the price of each book. I trusted him and finished the story of my life for him. After he published the book I wrote to him and ask [sic] him about the price which he promised me on the books he sold. He answered my letter and told me that there was another white man who has asked him to make this book so he himself hasn't seen a cent from the book which we made. By this I know he was deceiving me about the whole business. I also asked to put at the end of this story that I was not a pagan but have been converted into the Catholic Church in which I work as a catechist for more than 25 years. I've quit all these pagan works. But he didn't mention this. Cash talks. So if they can't put this religion life in the last part of that book, also if he can't pay what he promised, I ask you my dear friends that this book of my life will be null and void because I value my soul more than my body. I'm awful sorry for the mistake I made. I also have this witnesses [sic] to stand by me.
I'm yours truly
Nick Black Elk
my name is not Amerdian [sic] but he is lying about my name

Basing his evaluation of the above documents on correspondence between Ben Black Elk and Neihardt, DeMallie further noted the family's expressed respect for the author. (Ben even named a son after the poet.) Within this correspondence, mention is made of other catechists' being "opposed to—or perhaps jealous of—the book" (1984b:62), particularly one Emil Afraid of Hawk. Ben wrote that Emil "has been loading the old man about lots of things. The old man felt uneasy for a while. But he is perfectly satisfied, very glad to hear you are coming again." Given this information, DeMallie's conclusion regarding Lucy's involvement is a logical one. Other factors came into play, however, which Lucy painfully reported.

As mentioned earlier, there was some disagreement at the time of Neihardt's visit as to who his interpreter should be. According to Lucy, and corroborated by others, Emil's role as interpreter was short-lived, as Ben wished to have involvement with the project. Lucy's brother Ben thus became a moving force behind Neihardt's accumulation of data, but Lucy found herself at odds with her brother as to how the whole matter was being handled. Emil and Lucy dissociated themselves from the enterprise on grounds similar to those of the missionaries—that is, the highlighting of Black Elk's earlier years at the expense of his later ones.

Knowing of Ben's eagerness for further visits, and knowing about the above correspondence of Ben to Neihardt, Lucy would certainly advocate yet another declaration from her father (she made no reference to writing it herself). DeMallie recognized that the document was "difficult . . . to assess" and that "the motive for writing it is not clear." But given the date of the first declaration (January) and the date of Ben's invitation to Neihardt (June), and taking into consideration Lucy's resistance to her brother's involvement, it is not at all surprising that September finds Black Elk once again trying to clear the air. Unfortunate as this father-daughter-son interplay might be, it was nonetheless a reality Black Elk had to contend with during the book's writing and after its production.[5] In essence, the second letter is again Black Elk's, written in the midst of his children's disagreement. Appeasing both sides, the holy man seems to have ultimately steered a course that was as accommodating to as many parties as possible. A visit by Neihardt would be welcome, and Black Elk's identity as catechist would remain intact.

Who said what appears to have been a matter not easily laid to rest, since it also bore upon *Black Elk Speaks* itself. Joseph Epes Brown said in personal communication that while working on *The Sacred Pipe,* he had reason to correspond with John Neihardt, and that the poet insisted his depiction of Black Elk was greatly embellished and was only "based" on the holy man's recollections. (Supplementary material was apparently gleaned from other sources.) Similarly, instead of keeping the original title of his work, Neihardt requested in 1972 that it be changed to *Black Elk Speaks,* "as told *through*" the author. The 1932 edition had "as told *to*"—an important change that can be easily overlooked by readers. Nonetheless, in Brown's opinion, the book seemed greatly indebted to Black Elk. (Some Lakota, however, attribute much of the information to Ben.)

This publishing history, and the different perspectives that have accompanied it, is at times difficult to evaluate. However, one thing is clear. Lucy's father was not a stoic warrior preoccupied with a mythical past, nor was he an otherworldly mystic unconcerned with the pressing issues of everyday life. Instead, Lucy's account, combined with recollections of those who knew Black Elk, reveals the compelling personality captured in the Neihardt work and does so, simply, in a fashion that reads a little more down to earth.

The "forceful contortions" spoken of by Father Sialm were actually the prerogative of Neihardt in his choice of emphases. Whatever the poet may have embellished, whatever data he fictionalized into misleading or ambiguous con-

clusions regarding Black Elk's worldview, he still managed
to discover and reveal much of the substance that made the
holy man who he was. Before meeting Neihardt, Black Elk's
destiny as an internationally known mystic could only be
the imaginative dream of an old grandfather. After learning
about Black Elk's entire life from this more intimate perspective, however, one wonders if the disclosure of his story
from start to finish just might be a phenomenon not guided
solely by human design. It is indeed intriguing that a man's
vision still unfolds these long years after his death, revealed
to countless persons far removed from his place and time.

Consonant with Father Sialm's earlier remarks, Father
Zimmerman sent out a missionary appeal letter that em-
phasized Black Elk's role as catechist.

The Jesuit Fathers . . . trained him for his many years as a
catechist to his race—twenty-seven years on the Pine Ridge
Reservation—two years at Yankton Agency—one year at Sis-
seton Agency—and one year at St. Stephens, Wyoming,
among the Arapahos. His rare gift of making clear the
Catholic teachings won many inquirers. One of the old mis-
sionaries believes him responsible for at least four hundred
conversions. Old age, blindness and the seven miles be-
tween him and the nearest Catholic Church prevent him
from often hearing mass, so at times I promise to say mass
at his home. Then he sends out word and gathers in the
entire neighborhood, and as in his old time catechist days
leads them in hymns and prayers.

Reminiscent of the meeting between Neihardt and Black
Elk, Zimmerman recalled the holy man's greeting upon the
priest's return to Manderson after a three-year absence:
"Every day I saw you in my prayers. I knew you would
come back. When I looked and saw you, I could not believe
my eyes, and tears rolled down."[6]

In this same vein, Neihardt reported the following concerning his introduction to Black Elk: "'That was kind of funny, the way the old man seemed to know you were coming.' My son remarked that he had the same impression; and when I had known the great old man for some years I was quite prepared to believe that he did know, for he certainly had supernormal powers" (*BES*, x).

Lucy commented on Black Elk's ministry:

Once, after he retired, my father told me about the years when he first became a catechist. He said the people would scourge him with vicious words and make fun of him, since he had been a yuwipi medicine man. The people made a lot of vicious talk concerning him, but he held on and did not go back to his old ways.

There's a couple or three times, he said, that people would chase them out of the house—not wanting to have them in there. They belonged to this peyote clan (at that time they were really going strong). So they chased him out and even threw their books out. That's the kind of life he led, and those were some of the hardships he faced during his first years as a catechist.

My father told me: "At first, they called me names. They called me yuwipi man and said that I was the devil. But I was a catechist, so I never paid any attention to them. Pretty soon, they quieted down and started coming to me, working with me, and associating with me. I found out that the ones who did say those bad things about me were the ones most easily converted into the church. They'd come and talk to me and tell me this problem and that problem, and by just looking at their faces I could understand what kind of people they are in their hearts."

He said that "at first the little ones listened to me more than the older people. I was always willing to talk to them about God and about our Lord, who was born and died for all of us men. The little ones, the children, were really glad every time I had a service. They enjoyed it. It was the little children who were interested, who came, and listened to me. One of the greatest things God rewarded me with was the little ones. I was always loved by little ones. It seemed like God said, 'Let the children come to me' [see Luke 18:15-17], for that's the way it was. I still think that since I have become a grandfather, why I still am loved by little ones."

So that was always his main teaching. When he taught, he said, "Unless we become as children, become like those little children"—he would point to some—"we cannot enter the Kingdom" [Matt. 18:3]. That was his main topic.

Whenever they'd have a meeting—they always liked to have meetings at that time in the early life of the Sioux Catholics—they liked to hear about God and about Christianity. So they liked to have meetings. At that time, the regulations were very strict, so they didn't associate with the other denominations or have anything to do with divorced persons. They didn't allow them in the meetings.

At all Catholic gatherings—celebrations or meetings—they were bound to have my father lecture on something about the church. One of his favorite subjects was on the words "What does it profit a man if he gain the whole world and suffer the loss of his soul?" [Matt. 16:26]. That's one of the things I'll always remember about him teaching during those years.

My father would really stand out there preaching with all his might. He'd tell me, "It's pretty hard to be teaching the people. But still, I feel good when I get through. It seems I feel so good that I can just feel at ease when I finish instructing them—even though at first it's like doing heavy labor. Maybe Our Lord helps me to put on inspiring preaching."

I remember a relative of mine used to come over and used to gossip about her aunts and uncles. She used to talk about them and complain about them. So before she left one day, my father said to her, "Daughter-in-law, the strong person doesn't speak sharp words about their neighbor, or other persons. People hear such words and they like to hear them—

Black Elk speaking at Joe No Water's home, 1928. (Courtesy of the Buechel Memorial Lakota Museum.)

then they somehow feel satisfied. Seems like all they want to do is hear bad things."

My father gave her an example. He said: "It's like a dog who gets so hungry at times it goes out and gets all sorts of bones. Even if they're dry and rotted, he carries them back to the house and just piles them up stinking. The dog thinks there's real meat on the bones, he picks them up to eat— they're messy and not good for him at all. That's the way it is with people. They like to hear and speak harsh words all the time in all places."[7]

"You yourself, if you believe in God, should just forgive others. Don't mention anything about them. The people you complain about might just be ignorant. They themselves want to do good for you because they see you talk nice about them. They see you don't even care what they said to you. That way they'll be back in the religion and do things you respect. And when they're dead, you can say nice words about them."

That's what he told that lady. That's the way he talked— in a nice way so she wasn't offended. After my father said this to her, she was really getting along good with her relatives right up until they died.

When Lucy narrated her memories, the spirituality Black Elk imparted to her became more manifest, and a different perspective on the holy man gradually unfolded. The grandmother being interviewed was at one time a little girl—the dearly loved and only-born daughter of Black Elk's two marriages. Whatever religious practices or impulses Lucy possessed, and whatever spiritual sentiments she expressed, all were received through the counsel of her father. Black Elk's little girl, now a woman with grandchildren of her own, had clearly been the special recipient of her father's spiritual legacy—entrusted to her from birth and daily manifested within the context of household and reservation life.

▼

chapter seven

▼

Sacred Visions

In Lakota tradition, "visions of real significance could come to a child of ten and twelve years and might affect the course of his life" (Hassrick 1964:281). Never taken lightly by their recipients, such visions still retained a forceful hold on people quite advanced in age. A vision often prescribed particular obligations and brought special power to the person receiving it (Lowie 1963:170–75).

At the age of nine, Black Elk received a great vision, and Neihardt vividly narrates its details in an early chapter (*BES*, 17–39). Referred to as the living heart of the book and Black Elk's life, one commentary notes that an "attempt to describe it would do it injustice" (Waters 1984:187). *Seeing with a Native Eye*, a popular anthology of essays dealing with Indian religion, was even dedicated to the vision (Capps 1976).[1] This childhood experience is shown as haunting Black Elk's conscious life, and the holy man repeatedly asks of Wakan Tanka if he properly sought the vision's fulfillment. The book's concluding chapter mov-

93

ingly suggests that Wakan Tanka answered Black Elk's question affirmatively (231–34).

Cast in imagery typical of other Plains Indian visionary accounts, Black Elk's is difficult to comprehend. He himself spent a lifetime trying to actualize its promise. When DeMallie compared the stenographic record of Neihardt's vision interviews with what was presented in *Black Elk Speaks,* he found that a certain amount of condensation was effected, a few creative liberties taken, and clarity of interpretation elusive for both texts (1984b:94–99). Yet, a key to interpretation of the vision, perhaps unknown to Neihardt and other commentators, surfaced in Black Elk's life at the time of his conversion.

In an attempt to communicate Catholic theology nonabstractly, early missionaries made use of a picture catechism. On a strip of paper about one foot wide and several feet long were contained illustrations depicting what Christians have traditionally called salvation history. Goll described this mandalalike device as follows: "Beginning with the Blessed Trinity and Creation at the bottom of the strip, the student follows the connected pictures of God in heaven at the top. The Apostles Creed, the life and death of Christ, the Church, the sacraments, the theological virtues, the capital sins—all are there between two roads, a golden road leading to heaven and a black one ending in hell" (1940:30).[2] Native catechists were instructed as to the chart's meanings by means of individual and group lessons conducted by priests, and by written explanations in both English and Lakota.

Although differently drawn catechetical charts were employed by both Protestant and Catholic groups, the Two Roads Map (as it was popularly called) in use among the Lakota was a colorful, engaging depiction of human beings and preternatural creatures. The pantheon of Judeo-Christian figures is arresting, as winged angels and bat like demons are pictured fluttering about the course of world history. Crowds of people are variously portrayed—at the mercy of natural disaster, in the clutches of a leviathan monster, under the embrace of a grandfather-creator, and all in seemingly constant motion. In short, the Two Roads Map imaginatively captured in picture form the basic worldview of traditional Christian theology.[3]

Black Elk used the Two Roads Map during his life as a catechist, and many references within his vision correspond directly to the old picture catechism. Some of the surprising parallels include thunder beings, a daybreak star, flying men, tree imagery, circled villages, a black road, a red road, friendly wings, an evil blue man living in flames, a place where people moaned and mourned, emphasis on the people's history, and gaudily portrayed, self-indulgent individuals. Other, more detailed segments of Black Elk's vision are either explicitly or implicitly present on the Two Roads Map.

Psychologist Carl Jung (1970) highly regarded *Black Elk Speaks* and was particularly intrigued by the vision that Neihardt described. Had he known of the map's existence, Jung would have attributed the correspondence to humanity's "collective unconscious," that is, humanity's sharing of "a common, inborn, unconscious life inherited from the distant past, expressed in archetypal (universal) images and symbols" (Stauffer 1981:56).

Black Elk's closing utterances on Harney Peak allude to the picture catechism as he prays about his vision. He says to Wakan Tanka: "The good road and the road of difficulties you have made to cross; and where they cross, the place is holy" (*BES*, 232). These road references are made not just here but also in the earlier vision and later with Brown (1953:7n). However, all one can conclude from these isolated passages is that traditional Lakota could symbolize the virtuous life as being on a kind of "good red road," and evil behavior, or difficulties, as being on a black one.[4] Walker's turn-of-the-century interviews (1980:187, 189-90,

215, 232, 235) verify the color associations, but in Black Elk's case much more obtains.

That the good-evil dualism is found on the Two Roads Map is not particularly noteworthy. More important is the color symbolism and the notion of good and evil roads. Running the length of the map is a "way of good" and a "way of evil," both of which intermittently touch the map's center. The roadlike center section is directional, with the black rungs on the lower half representing the centuries before Christ, and the red ones on the upper half the centuries after him. In light of these depictions, Black Elk's references seem to take on additional meaning.

According to both the vision and the map, the forces of evil have always contended with those of good. The vision's repetitive references to red, and red's association with the good, make the map's Christ-event critical. That is, the map's red section is identified with the Christian era. It seems to be the path Black Elk prays his people might find and follow.

In Neihardt's unedited transcript, Black Elk is reported as describing his vocation in terms that are clearly compatible with both the map and his long years of labor as a catechist. He says: "I had been appointed by my vision to be an intercessor of my people. . . . I'd bring my people out of the black road into the red road. From my experience and from what I know, and in recalling the past from where I was at that time I could see that it was next to impossible, but there was nothing like trying. Of course probably the Spirit world will help me" (DeMallie 1984b:293). Given the imagery at work here, (i.e., from the black-colored, pre-Christian era into the red-colored Christian era), Black Elk's self-understanding was clearly that of a leader of his people into Christian times.

Black Elk's conversion, along with his work as a catechist, was embraced as a more sober life-trajectory than the feverish activity that accompanied his Ghost Dance involvement. The Messiah Craze might then be seen as a kind of theological transition period. It served as a prelude to Black Elk's later acceptance of a belief system that bore concepts with which he was already familiar. Moreover, presented pictorially, the earlier vision was coherently ratified by being placed in a more global context. Whatever its definitional shortcoming, Neihardt's emphasis on such universal concepts as right conduct, human harmony, peace, and friendship was in fact an accurate reflection of themes within Black Elk's vision. The vision was, however, enhanced by the substance of a salvation history that was succinctly delineated on the Two Roads Map.[5]

A patent difference between the vision and the map is that the north-south red road and the west-east black road of Black Elk's vision do not bisect one another on the catechetical chart. The map's two roads appear as distinct routes separated by illustrations of Christ's life. (Interestingly, though, the vision imagery depicts these roads in the form of a cross.) So too, the map's black section is not strictly designated as one of troubles, any more than the red road is designated as good (even though "good," or "better," would be implied as the Christian era eclipses its prehistory). Finally, the catechism's specifically marked paths of good and evil never intersect with the red and black sections.

Nonetheless, reflecting on his vision in later life, Black Elk's comments to Neihardt sound as if he might just as well have been talking about the Two Roads Map and the instructions he received concerning it. In Black Elk's words, "It was the pictures I remembered and the words that went with them. . . . It was as I grew older that the meanings came clearer and clearer out of the pictures and the words; and even now I know that more was shown to me than I can tell" (*BES*, 41).[6] Why Neihardt asked Black Elk's friend Standing Bear to sketch pictures of the vision is difficult to understand, as they are not Black Elk's and are in fact distracting. Instead, if the Two Roads Map had been included, this present discussion would have been started years ago.

A comparison of the map and the vision could become a lengthy study in itself. In fact, the temptation exists to find a complete one-to-one correspondence between the two. Yet, although the vision of the picture catechism and Black Elk's private vision are similar, enough different nuances exist to cause some hesitation in seeing things that actually might not be present (especially since he might have taught from maps that, though closely resembling one another, had varying details). Ultimately, though, the propositions here are supported by recollections of Lucy and acquaintances of Black Elk.

Maybe Neihardt unknowingly transcribed Black Elk's description of the map as the latter blended into it an earlier vision or clothed it in Lakota imagery. Perhaps Black Elk condensed a number of visions and used as an inspirational force the Two Roads Map, from which he taught for three decades. Or did time simply obscure the vision he once had, so that the holy man wove into his account some elements from the catechism? Comparison of the two requires the reconstruction of such possibilities.

When Brown visited Black Elk, he found that the holy man was still haunted by his vision, whatever its source (1953:xv). Neihardt did not fabricate its impact. As was common in Lakota society, Black Elk had received a vision, and it provided him an abiding sense of mission.

Black Elk's poignant religious experience during boyhood set him in quest of its fulfillment. Years later, after much heartbreak and disappointment, he found himself doctoring a dying child near Payabya. The encounter with Father Lindebner and subsequent exposure to the strangely familiar picture catechism confirmed in what direction the rest of his life would lead. Black Elk's vision seems to have been a foreshadowing of what was later amplified *via* Ghost Dance themes and the Two Roads Map. Whether this ultimately is a case of mysticism, clairvoyance, creative imagination, fiction, or coincidence remains an engaging speculation that will never be confirmed.

Although charting the cognitive patterns at work in Black Elk's life is somewhat speculative, the suggestions here seem likely. If the vision was reported accurately, its similarity to the picture catechism underscored its prophetic place within Black Elk's life. Whether the Neihardt account is Black Elk's superimposition of the map on his vision (or vice versa) will probably never be known for sure; if some blending occurred, however, it was done so because Black Elk regarded the two as part of a continuum. The accounts that follow reveal Black Elk's vision as he came to interpret it, one whose entire meaning could be understood only in light of the Two Roads Map.

Lucy described the map as follows:

I remember Ate Ptecela used to bring a kind of map—with a red road and a yellow road on it. And my father taught me what it was—the good road and the bad road. He would pray, "Canku wan luta akan napata—on the red road we want to walk—I, my relatives, my children, and grandchildren." He learned the idea of the black road when he was a catechist.

One time Father Lindebner came and said "Lucy, let me see what you learned about this map." Right away I rolled it out and said, "Father, sit down. I'm going to teach you something." My father had taught me about it, and I was really good at telling about it.

In the words of Ben Marrowbone:

Black Elk used the Two Roads Map to teach the old people. He would show that in the beginning, God created every-

Two Roads Map, like the one used by Black Elk. Such maps were used at Pine Ridge as early as 1911. Printed by Catholic Press, Ranchi, India. 8" x 36". (From the collection of Michael F. Steltenkamp. Photo by Tudor Studio.)

Black Elk using the Two Roads Map to instruct children,
ca. 1935. (Courtesy of the Buechel Memorial Lakota Museum.)

*thing. And then all these pictures would help them under-
stand easier. He would teach the old people about the seven
sacraments, and that cross. Crucified, hanged between
heaven and earth, was the Son of God.*

*So on every church you see a cross—great worship. This
is why Christ came: to build his church on a rock of strength,
to stand in place of him. Nick Black Elk explained this
church to the people—this great church. He explained and
they understood.*

John Lone Goose also reflected on the map.

*He'd teach them that map many times. He carried one. So
everytime we go teach, he'd go down the Two Roads. He
taught them how to go to heaven and how to be a Christian
man. On another road, they would go to hell.*

*Father gave him a Two Roads Map, and he taught from
it the rest of his life. One road was black and is the devil.
The other is yellow—the very good road to heaven. He'd
show the people that some go this way, and some go the
black road. Some people believed it and turned around and*

became a catechist. He turned lots of souls to our Lord away from hell.

If he took it in his grave, I don't know. I didn't see that road map any more after he died.

Lucy tried to explain some of the parallels between Christianity and traditional Lakota religion that she and her father recognized.

He and Father Buechel would talk. They talked about my father's visions . . . and the Sun Dance, and all the Indian ceremonies that my father said were connected to Christianity. My father said we were like the Israelites, the Jews, waiting for Christ. And some Jews didn't want to accept Jesus as God.

He said all these ceremonies connected. They knew, somehow, that in the future our Lord Jesus Christ would come one day to his people. Well, actually they didn't see him, but he did come. And the missionaries brought the teachings of Our Lord. They knew, somehow, in the future they would learn this. And they somehow already practiced it in the Sun Dance. That's the way he took it.

Like they say, "Pagan way, adoring the sun"—but it's not that. He told me. They pray and say to the Great Spirit, "Without any sinful thoughts or actions, we're going to do this for you." That's the way they feel when they do these Sun Dance ceremonies. They purify themselves—that's why they wear the sage crown, which resembles the crown our Lord wore—and they start dancing. So the Indian, early before sunrise, had to stand there and had to go with the sun— watching it until it went down. That's the suffering, you see. And some of them even shed their blood. Christ did that too, before he died on the cross. That was the way he suffered.[7]

No woman was allowed to go near because Eve was the first one to come with sin. That's why women were behind the men and weren't allowed to take part in the Sun Dance.

But I don't know if my father totally understood it that way.
Only one place could a woman be a part of it, and she had
to be a virgin.

This Sun Dance made them suffer from sunup till sun-
down. They prayed to the Great Spirit and suffered from
fasting for three days and not drinking water. Our Lord
fasted forty days. They want the Great Spirit to accept their
sacrifice because what they want to do is for the sake of
their people, for their sick ones, for a richer life, enough to
eat, and enough health. That's the way they pray, so the
Great Spirit will watch and take care of them.

So Christianity, they already did practice it—in a way that
wasn't really too much against the rules of the church. Of
course, there were a lot of ceremonies along with it—like the
fathers have Masses and all these special days and celebra-
tions. But still, my father was pretty much the new religion.

Central to the spirituality of the Lakota, in particular,
was a sacred pipe *(cannunpa wakan)*. Use of this ritual
instrument was a crucial feature of every religious ceremony, which Brown well reported in his work with Black
Elk. Calling so special an object simply a peace pipe, as is
often done, is a misnomer.

A legend well known to the Lakota says that Buffalo Cow
Woman (a heavenly, mysterious, and beautiful lady) came
many generations ago, bearing what appeared to be a child.
In the course of events, however, the bundle she brought
was unwrapped and found to hold the Sacred Calf Pipe. As
time passed, the holy lady revealed how the pipe was to be
used and the seven rites that were to be observed by the
people. Furthermore, all subsequent pipe usage was to
recall this special revelation. Regarded as a particularly
sacred and unique gift, a ritual pipe became synonymous
with Lakota religious practice. (Small pipes were used for
leisurely occasions.) It ensured the people of communication with Wakan Tanka.[8]

Among the early missionaries, attitudes concerning the pipe varied, paralleling the thought of modern Lakota people themselves. Some regarded the pipe as a sacred symbol within the religious heritage, while others saw it as dysfunctional in the twentieth-century world. Arguments regularly arise today in Native contexts pitting Christian tradition (or even peyote tradition) against the pipe tradition; one group or another typically has members who cannot reconcile the blend (Steltenkamp 1982:21–49).[9] The accounts that follow can contribute to further discussion in such circles.

According to Ben Marrowbone:

A heavenly woman once came and gave us a pipe. Every family had to keep a pipe of its own—use it every day, at night too. That woman gave it to us and told us to talk to the Almighty—pray for whatever we need—for rain or good crops. You didn't have to see any great vision. The Almighty hears you. Take this pipe. Pray that he hears you. That's what the holy woman said. That kind of order was given our grandfathers. So they followed.

Before he converted, Nick Black Elk talked to Almighty God with that pipe. He learned that the same God talked to white people. That's why those catechists believed in the Catholic church. Nobody said: "Oh, you fool you!" No. That's the great Almighty you are respecting and honoring—in a new way. And just as we were brought the sacred pipe, we now had the sacred bread [i.e., the Eucharist] from heaven.

Nick Black Elk used to use that pipe in his wapiya [curing ceremony], and he believed in it. At that time there weren't any doctors, so different ceremonies were used for healing. So I think Black Elk worked according to the Almighty. These old people used this pipe and prayed to one Spirit. That was their foundation. That's what they said.

The catechists would get together, have meetings, encourage each other—show interest in one another. At one such gathering, Nick Black Elk stood up and said: "Yuwipi come from Santee. We have a pipe here. We use that. God gave us that pipe from heaven through a woman. Two young men met her while out hunting. One of them had bad thoughts about her and was punished. But the other one was a good man. She told him, 'I want to explain to the Lakota people how to pray.' She brought that pipe and gave it to an old man—a good man with a good conscience.

"That pipe—it's a road to take—a road of honesty—a road to heaven. It teaches how to lead a good life, like the Ten Commandments. They understood what that woman was saying, and that worship was my formation—my foundation. But my foundation is deepening.

"God made me to know him, love him, serve him. To make sure I do this, God sent us his Son. The old way is good. God prepared us before the missionary came. Our ancestors used the pipe to know God. That's a foundation! But from the old country came Christ from heaven—a wonderful thing—the Son of God. And the Indian cares about this.

"This is not our home. Our home is the new world coming. We come here, lead a good life, and follow the good road. That's the only way to save ourselves and see our relatives again. This body goes, but the spirit keeps on. And if we take the right road, try and lead a good life, be honest, and live as brothers in one relationship, we will see our relatives. We will see God our relative. The evil spirit is against what I say. The evil spirit is like Iktomi, who fools people."[10]

This Nick Black Elk, he was kind of a young fellow. He had catechist instruction. And one brother—his name was Brother Graf—taught him Indian songs like Jesus Cante.[11] So Nick picked up some young fellows and taught them some songs—church songs. And these young fellows learn quickly. They can think without Bible. Word spread that "Black Elk is going to teach the boys church songs, Catholic songs." So while these boys went into the tepee and sang,

Left to right: Catechists Max Bald Eagle, John Kills at Lodge, and Nicholas Black Elk, 1927. (Courtesy of the Buechel Memorial Lakota Museum.)

the people laid on their backs outside just listening. That was the first time they introduced religious songs.

Lucy also commented on her father's pipe, as well as his teaching.

He didn't have a pipe until after he was retired from his missionary work. They used to have a little pipe, which he and my mother used to smoke, and he was never keeper of the Sacred Calf Pipe. He used his own when he prayed to the Great Spirit—nothing else. He never did tell me about the meaning of the pipe. He'd just say it was something that was given to them, so it was supposed to be sacred. You pray with it.

I think it was at the first Sun Dance in 1928 that my father met Elk Head. He came over to our camp and my mother told me, "Don't go in front of this man. He's the one that had the pipe, that sacred pipe." And here my father said: "Shake hands with him." So I shook hands with him. And today they keep that pipe up in Green Grass.

I think we accepted that pipe from the Great Spirit through a sacred lady who brought it to all the human beings. We say that we Christian women should be like her. She told the people that a man who has the pipe should pray with it.

Just like commandments, she told them that men should be peaceful men, nice men. There should be no quarrels or arguments, no committing any kind of adultery, and no feelings to criticize. The Great Spirit created all things through his power, so man has to love all the creatures—even the trees. This is what the Pipe Lady instructed. Father Buechel accepted the Blessed Virgin as the same one who brought the pipe, and that was what we always thought.

Apart from these references relating to his vision and the pipe, Black Elk's comments about a sacred tree are perhaps most familiar to readers of the Neihardt material. At the end of *Black Elk Speaks,* the holy man is pictured looking back on his life and tearfully saying to Wakan Tanka that "the tree has never bloomed" (*BES,* 233). He goes on to plead: "It may be that some little root of the sacred tree still lives. Nourish it then, that it may leaf and bloom and fill with singing birds" (233). Besides this famous passage, the unedited manuscript contains repeated references to the tree.

The account is emotionally powerful, as it depicts Black Elk as a man whose vision would die with him. Readers presume the holy man's references are to the rebirth of a tribal past that is no more and are moved to feel the sadness Black Elk speaks. As DeMallie observes (1984b:56): "With its unrelenting sense of defeat," the book (and especially its conclusion) "became an eloquent literary restatement of the theme of the vanishing American."

However, Lucy was insistent that her father did not speak out of sadness, as these passages implied. Her tone was matter-of-fact as she attempted to communicate the meaning of his references.

The following section also includes Lucy's tradition-based understanding of her Lakota courtship and marriage. (For background, see chapter 1.) On this subject, her comments are typical of the older generation, while seldom, if ever, heard among younger people. Curiously enough, recent evidence suggests that marriage between cousins is on the rise and is no longer associated with a disaster-bearing taboo (DeMallie 1979).

Given the content of the following passage, it should also be noted that, historically, Lakota acceptance of Christianity initially fell within Roman Catholic, Episcopalian, and Presbyterian traditions. These three remain the dominant groups, in spite of subsequent exposure to other denominations. As elsewhere nowadays, and in contrast to the religious sparring of earlier generations, ecumen-

Lucy Black Elk
wearing a woman's
hairpipe breastplate,
1928. (Courtesy of the
Buechel Memorial
Lakota Museum.)

ism has grown over the years, and a spirit of interde-
nominational cooperation for the common good has been
fostered.[12]

In Lucy's words:

*The Great Spirit has promised one day that the tree of my
father's vision was to root, grow, and blossom—to give out its
flourishing sweet scent for everyone, and become a symbol
of life. I know this. He meant it's like the Catholic faith. Our
Lord told St. Peter to establish the religion just like that. The
Great Spirit gave the Sioux people a knowledge of Christianity through the sacred pipe. But this tree would grow and
spread out strong, flowing branches. He had that vision and
learned the tree was to be the Christian life of all people.*

Black Elk, holding prayer book, in right front pew of St. Elizabeth's church, Oglala, South Dakota, 1936. (Courtesy of the Bureau of Catholic Indian Missions.)

At the time before he died, he had a sad tale. He said he didn't do his part in accomplishing this and that the tree was dying. People were not walking the right path. But he still hoped the tree would be able to give forth its branches before it was entirely dead. I know this is what he meant.

The time I got married to Leo was on August 18, 1929, at St. Agnes Chapel—since my father wanted me to be married in the church. I had to marry this man because he did a lot of favors for my folks since they were old. He used to go over there, cut wood, and haul water for them. We had to get water from the creek. My husband had been an Episcopal, so I thought, "If you like him enough, okay, but he has to become a Catholic," so he went and joined the Catholic faith before our wedding. Our celebrating priest was Father Sialm, S.J., and my father was real happy afterward. He honored us by giving a big dinner, or reception.

From this marriage we had ten children, but during the depression we lost six boys.[13] So there are just four surviving now. Leo's grandfather was related to my mother—a cousin—so I'm a first or second cousin to Leo's father. I think that's why we've had tragedy in our family—because we're blood related. A tough life both of us had, but he's now resting in peace.[14] The only disappointing thing is that my father and mother didn't see my grandchildren. My father and mother died before my children grew up. But my father did see my brother Ben's grandchildren. He saw three of them, so I know he was happy to see four genera-tions of Black Elks.

▼

chapter eight

▼

Elder

Following his retirement from church work, Black Elk restricted his activity to more leisurely pursuits during warm weather months. He took particular pleasure in mixing with tourists who flocked to the Rapid City area. His son Ben later assumed such a role and became well known to visitors who toured the Mount Rushmore region.

This summer involvement was a welcome and enjoyable reprieve from the sweltering sameness of summer life on the reservation. Sociable by nature, the old medicine man-turned-catechist was delighted to appear in public with his grandson and to reenact scenes of traditional Lakota life at Duhamel's Sioux Indian Pageant, one of the area's popular tourist attractions. DeMallie speculated that Black Elk's motivation for doing "these sacred rituals appears to have been to teach white audiences that the old-time Lakota religion was a true religion, not devil worship as the missionaries claimed" (1984b:66). If such an underlying reason prompted her father's participation, Lucy was not aware of it. According to her, it "was just a show . . . he never really meant it." The pageant was, rather, an opportunity for her dad to get out in his old age. Furthermore, it was a way for him to "get more side money for the pictures they took of him."

Meanwhile, younger catechists were now undertaking responsibilities formerly handled by Black Elk. They passed on, as best they could, the religious tenets he preached for so many years. Since it was customary for older persons to be guest speakers at special assemblies (still a time-honored practice), Black Elk was now accorded this privilege. He accepted such invitations with enthusiasm.

Elders in fact had few responsibilities, and Neihardt depicted this by saying the holy-man and his friends had little to do "but wait for yesterday." Poetic characterizations aside, the senior generation did have occasion to reminisce nostalgically about their younger days, and Black Elk's granddaughter vividly recalled these gatherings. In his declining years, the holy man was not burdened with household chores and so was free to visit families whose ancestors he had known from another age. A revered catechist and elder, he was welcome wherever he went. He lived through the "old days" and helped forge a new life for others in the reservation era. Nick Black Elk was a special guest at homes, and the people knew he would not be theirs much longer. Lucy recounts:

After he quit being a catechist and had time of his own, he wanted to join in recreational activities. For instance, one time there was a dance being held at the house of one of his older friends. They didn't use to have meeting halls like they do now, so dances were held at homes. Anyway, he wanted to go to that dance real badly. My mother didn't want to go, and I didn't either because I was pregnant at the time. I wouldn't go in that wagon for anything.

Finally, my husband talked about going, and my father said: "We can saddle a horse and we'll ride together. I'll

ride on the back." So they both did. It was quite a sight
to see because my father wore his Indian costume to that
dance. There he was—behind my husband on that horse.
As soon as he got on, my father kicked the horse, and it got
spooked and started running with my husband and him on
it. He let out a whoop like in the old times—hollering out like
a cowboy. His little bells were jingling and ringing all the
way. My father yelled out: "We're going to fall," but Leo
shouted, "Hang on, father-in-law, I don't want you to fall
off!" Later on, my mother got after my father and said:
"You could have got hurt."[1]

In about 1936, he started working for Alex Duhammel at
the Sitting Bull Cave on Highway 16.[2] There was a show-
place where they put on a pageant for tourists, and my
father had a main part in it—as medicine man. The pageant
would show him doctoring a little boy (which was my son
Georgie), preparing a death scaffold, and leading the Sun
Dance. He would also pray with the pipe and smoke it. But
it was just a show, and he never meant it. The women got a
dollar and a quarter, and the men got a dollar and a half. It
was during depression, but they made quite a bit of money
on his performance.

My father was a good friend of Gutzon Borglum, too,
and he and Georgie would perform for crowds at Mount
Rushmore while it was still not finished.[3] After they finished carving Lincoln, they had a big dedication because
Lincoln was the last one. My father went up there in a cable
car with my sister-in-law's sister and my boy. They were all
dressed in Indian, and my father sang up there on top of
Lincoln's head. But by 1947, he was too old to continue
doing this work.

My mother died February 19, 1941, and my father took it
hard for awhile afterward. They lived northwest of Oglala
at the time, so he moved back to Manderson to stay with
Ben or my brother Nick's family or myself. On the Decoration Day [i.e., Memorial Day] after she died, my father was

asked to preach at the cemetery. Of course, he was now getting old, so he wasn't really strong. Anyway, he spoke out under the sun for too long a time, because when we brought him back home he collapsed. But that's the way he was. Even though he retired, he would still occasionally give a speech—a good one too.

Families still assemble in great numbers on Memorial Day to care for the graves of deceased relatives. Generally, such a gathering has a priest present who conducts a prayer service or celebrates a Mass for all in attendance. A "feed" follows this annual ceremony, so the day is quite a social occasion. Black Elk was a regular participant in these activities.

The *Indian Sentinel* reported the death of Black Elk's wife in a two-page obituary of November 1941. The following excerpts parallel Lucy's recollection of her parents.

Brings White was a strong and active member of the St. Mary's Society and set an attractive example of what a Catholic woman should be. . . . Even during these last few years, when both Black Elk and Brings White have been enfeebled by age and illness, their home has been a kind of mission center where the Sioux in the neighborhood gather to pray and sing hymns. Whether it was a tent or a cabin, it has always been a welcome home for the missionary.

On one occasion, Father Henry Westropp drove up to the church at St. Agnes Mission rather late. In those days the missionaries made their rounds by means of horses and buggies, often travelling many miles and sometimes reaching their destination after everyone had gone to bed. Father Westropp stopped his team a few feet from Brings White's tent and as usual shouted out: Tunwin, *meaning "Aunt." This awakened Brings White, who, recognizing the voice, called back,* Han mitoska, *meaning, "Yes, my nephew."*

Again, Father cheerfully spoke out: Tunwin, wanagi ki

palek cek ama u pelo, *meaning, "Aunt, the ghosts have pushed me here." . . . Father Westropp knew that this expression would amuse his hostess. He always had something clever to say. This is why the Indians called him Little Owl.*

Brings White, of course, was always delighted to receive her "nephew" and, regardless of the hour, would prepare a real Sioux meal for her visitor. All the interesting and amusing stories which had been collected by both since the last visit were told and sometimes all would laugh themselves to sleep.

I am reminded of all this, because just lately good old Brings White passed away peacefully to her reward. Though her death caused great sorrow to Black Elk and her children and many friends, they were consoled by her faith and piety as she received the Holy Food for the last time and the Sacrament of the dying.

The *Sentinel* carried a photograph of Black Elk's wife and family. The reporter was Stephen McNamara, S.J., a priest whose work began at Pine Ridge in 1928.

The catechist's last years left a legacy of impressions. One type of incident was especially recalled by the family and was similar to what is perhaps the most memorable sketch in Neihardt's work. The postscript concluding *Black Elk Speaks* presents a striking example of the holy man's peculiar relationship to nature. He is portrayed as asking for a sign of encouragement, and in the end he receives it. He says it will rain if Wakan Tanka hears his prayer, and it does rain—in a time of drought. Curiously enough, this sort of occurrence is heard in discussions related to the pipe's power in controlling weather.[4] Lucy's account below is representative of the genre.

My daughter Regina always remembers how often my father would go outside and look up at the sky. He would rub his hair backward saying, "Hey, hey, hey, hey," and would know if a storm was coming—even if the sky was all blue. It would come if he said it would.

And that reminds me of the time we were going to have a bad storm—a big thunderstorm. It looked like it was going to have a tornado in it. We didn't have a cellar, only a small grain house to hide in. My father was a pretty old man at the time.

He took his pipe upon a hill and stood facing the west. He then sang this song.

> A Thunderbird, that is the nation! (Three times)
> The people, you are alive!
> A nation that will live well!

After he was finished, you should have seen those clouds. One went off this way, one off that way, and the storm was gone. They must have heard him.

My father must have sung that around my kids because one time we went to town and left my oldest daughter with my in-laws. They put her in the big house and called another uncle of Leo's to go and sit with her. When he arrived, he heard her singing that song. And here the thunder and the wind stopped. We laughed when we heard about that.

My father was a patient man, and sometimes I compare him with my father-in-law, who was just the opposite. He would crab at everything as he got older. But my father never complained. My father was happy all the time. You can see how my father-in-law's son is taking after his father.[5]

My father still liked to visit other people. Even though he retired from his catechist work, he liked to go to sick people and pray for them. If anybody died in a family, he'd visit that family and speak with them and console them. He did a lot of that even though he was retired.

When our family would get together on Thanksgiving Day, my father used to say this prayer. I remember it:

I am talking to you, Grandfather Great Spirit, on this day.
Pitifully, I sit here.
I am speaking for my relatives, my children,
      my grandchildren, and all my
      relatives—wherever they might be.
Hear me, Grandfather, Great Spirit.

With your help, our needs are taken care of.
You have helped us in the time of want during the past.
And on this day we wish to thank you.
Hear me, O Great Spirit.
This day is a day of thanksgiving.
The nations of living things the world
      over—and we the two-leggeds, along with the
      children and the smaller ones with them—come
      to you today to express thanks.

In the future, make us see again a red day of good.
In the past, you have preserved us from evil
      on this red road.
Keep us on this road, and do not let us see anything wrong.

I, my children, and my grandchildren shall
      walk—led like children by your hand.
You have helped us in all things.
And Grandfather, Great Spirit, through your power
      alone we have survived.

Grandfather, Great Spirit, you have come and
      put us down—gathered together on mother
      earth.
And while we continue in this world, you provide food
for all living creatures.
So we give you thanks on this day.
Grandfather,
Take pity on me.

One day, we shall go and arrive at the end of
      the road.

In that future, we shall be without any sin
   at all.
And so it will be in the same manner for my
grandchildren and relatives who will follow as well.
We give you thanks, Grandfather
Great Spirit.
I am sending this prayer to you.[6]

Lucy's daughter Norma recalled these childhood memories of her grandfather.

After I grew up and went to school, I found out my grandfather was pretty famous. He was an important person, but I remember when I was a small girl he had a lot of time for me. We used to have a real small place, and my parents made him sleep on a bed while my brother and I slept on the floor. He'd say to me: "If you want to sleep on this bed, crawl in." So I always crawled in with him. He always felt sorry for me.

My grandfather always used to babysit for us when my parents went out, so I'd say to him lots of times: "I want to ride a horse." So he'd catch our horse named Brownie, put a halter on it, and set me on top. He'd take me all over these hills. And while he led the horse, he was either always reciting his prayer book or saying the rosary.

Real old men would come to the house and sit on the floor in a circle telling stories and smoking. They used old Indian words that I couldn't understand, but I would sit with them all the time next to my grandfather. He might have been a famous person because of those books he wrote, but I always remember him being around me and concerned about me until he died.

Georgie [Norma's brother] remembers when my parents bought him a tricycle, my grandfather would watch over him as he rode it. My grandfather had a cane, and he'd watch Georgie to see that he stayed on the road. If he went off the road, my grandfather would hook the wheel with his

Black Elk with the Scabby Face family he instructed, 1945.
(Courtesy of the Buechel Memorial Lakota Museum.)

*cane and make him go straight. He'd pray as he did that
too.*[7]

The grandparents of today were young adults toward the
end of Black Elk's life, yet old enough to understand why
his presence commanded respect. Their religious instruction was administered by younger catechists and priests a
generation removed from the holy man, whose boyhood
friends were gradually disappearing. One such present-
day elder remembers Black Elk as walking from his house
to church every Sunday (a distance of two miles), walking
stick in hand, and needing help to rise from the Communion rail as infirmity took its toll.

Pat Red Elk, another long-standing member of the community, was a young man during this period, and his account is representative of others from his age group.

*Even though they didn't have any formal education, those
old converts were really trained to preach. They'd say that
Saint John says this here and there, and when I'd get the*

The Catholic Sioux Indian Congress, 1946. Black Elk is fourth
from right in top row.

Bible and read it—they were right! That's what was writ-
ten. I read Scripture, but I can't remember the right words
like they used to be able to do. Yes, those old converts could
really talk—especially about religion. And they'd just
really give you the works! They really knew what to say.

Nick was a catechist, and when he got up he really
preached. People sat there and just listened to him. They
could picture what he was talking about. I remember one
time when he was pretty old, he really bore down on them.
He said: "The older people who constructed and kept up
the church are all fading away . . . and the new generation
isn't continuing the work that the people did. When I come to
church in wintertime, there's no firewood in that little box
there [he'd point to the woodbox], and tears come to my
eyes." Nowadays we have education, but we're not that good.

On Sunday morning you'd see Nick walking down the
road from where Ben lived—two, three miles outside of Man-
derson. In wintertime he didn't hardly come—too cold. But

summertime, spring, and fall, he'd be walking. He was old, so he got an early start and wouldn't catch a ride. And every Sunday, he'd join up with John Lone Goose right around where the store is now, and they'd say the rosary together. One would begin and say "Hail Mary." The other would finish the prayer. By the time they got to church, they had said the whole thing.[8]

Despite ill health, Black Elk lived out his remaining days in the same contemplative spirit that characterized his earlier life. Having confronted death in other, more dramatic contexts, the holy man was now resigned to await patiently its final visit. What restlessness he experienced came in the form of physical discomfort, in particular, a stroke that his aged cousin, Little Warrior, was instrumental in relieving.

The Lakota word for stroke is *wanagiktepi*, a literal translation of which is "killed by ghosts"—an etymology that conveys the perceived seriousness of the condition. Little Warrior's skill reflects the rich tradition of healing ceremonies developed by the Lakota. Home remedies are still used in modern reservation households (Steltenkamp 1982:129–32; Vogel 1970).

Lucy speaks further of her father's health.

One day, in the spring of 1948, it was really slippery. My father went outside, lost his footing, fell, and broke his hip. He was around eighty then, and from that time until his death he was bedridden. We put him in a wheelchair when he wanted to sit up or go outside. And after that happened, he said he was ready to accept his Creator's call any time. But for me, he said I should try and carry on the works of the church and go to Mass very often.

When he had that accident, he tried to argue with me, saying he was alright. But we took him to the hospital anyway. While he was there his tuberculosis caused him some

trouble but not serious. He caught that when he was young.
He also had a stroke while there and was given the last rites
for the third time in his life. The second time was when he
was sick.

Anyway, he recovered and came to stay here at our house.
Even though he couldn't walk, he still prayed and sang.
There was never a day he complained about his suffering.
He'd sit praying and he'd tell us, "Never fail to miss a day
without your prayers. God will take care of you and reward
you for this. Say the rosary too, because that is one of the
powerful prayers of Our Lord's mother." That's how he was.

He was uncomfortable at our house because it was so small
and hot during the summer. So he asked if he could go back
to the hospital, where it was cooler. That's when he moved to
my brother Ben's house, where he stayed until he died.

At times, I'd just go over to him and try to make him feel
good. He got to be so blind that he couldn't read his Indian
prayer books, but he had learned them by heart. He seemed
to always have a rosary in his hands, and even though he
was sick, you'd never hear him complain. When he came to
stay at our place, we had to pray. He never forgot.

Joseph Epes Brown also used to tell of Black Elk's insistence on prayer. While in Denver, the two men stopped at a
diner. In this very nonreligious environment, patrons were
noticeably dumbstruck to witness the aged holy man pray
aloud before eating. The Indian prayer book Lucy recalls
her father memorizing was *Sursum Corda: Lakota Woce-*
kiye na Olowan Wowapi (Sioux Indian Prayer and Hymn
Book), a compact little book of 386 pages published by the
Central Bureau of the Catholic Central Verein of America,
in St. Louis, Missouri. Lucy continues:

When my father was released from the sanatorium and was
well enough to stay at our home, he was also partially par-
alyzed. His mouth was crooked due to the stroke, and he

had trouble eating. So, as I said, I used to sit down and talk to him to make him feel better, because he was all by himself.

One day I asked him: "Dad, I wonder if this man you call your cousin would be able to bring you out of this stroke?" You see, before my father got crippled, he used to often talk with a man named Little Warrior—and this is who I meant. Little Warrior was a Catholic and did wanagi wapiya [ghost ceremony of healing]. And he was good at that, they told me.

My father didn't really want this, but he had respect for his cousin and myself, so he agreed to go through with it. I called my brother Ben, who was really after this kind of thing—curious about it too—and we arranged to have it at my house. We prepared the sweatlodge, but my father didn't go in—just three older men. He didn't want that doctoring done on him [whereas Ben wanted more exposure to the older tradition].

When we were ready to have that ceremony, Little Warrior said: "You know these other types of medicine men and yuwipi men—they always tell you to close the windows so there will be dark. They tell you to take down from the wall the holy pictures and rosary. I say no. Those are the ones we are going to pray to. Just watch that rosary while this is going on. If you have a rosary, you'd better say it while I'm doctoring your father." That's what Little Warrior said about our picture of the Sacred Heart and this big rosary we had on the wall.[9]

Well, I must have really believed him, because I took my rosary and sat there saying it. Pretty soon, the main time comes for those little spirits to doctor my father. All at once, I'm in the middle of my rosary and I remember what Little Warrior had told me. So I looked up at our rosary on the wall, and you ought to have seen those little things on each bead. Those little lights—there must be a bunch of them— were all glowing on the beads. And that cross, it just glowed.

And the holy picture—the sacred picture—those little things just sat around it. I think they were worshiping the picture.

I noticed after everything was over that my father's mouth had straightened out, so he could eat. Before that, I had a hard time feeding him. My father, after it was all over, said to Little Warrior: "Yes, I'll admit you're good at it. But next time you come to doctor me, don't let those little spirits treat me so roughly. They were really treating me harsh. I'm really tired." Mind you, his mouth was straight and he could eat after that ceremony.

And that's when I got confused. I asked my father: "Why in the world—how is it that you became a Catholic cate-chist?" Then he told me about his conversion. I had heard the story when I was in the teen age, but I never paid any attention to it. So I was a little older when he explained these things to me. It was after I got married, then I realized and understood these things about my father.

Little Warrior told me: "In my life, there are good spirits and bad spirits. When you pray, the good spirit is always going to help you. In the morning, when you get up, stand in the doorway and pray that the day is a nice quiet day. Give thanks for the day—for coming through the night." I guess he was glad that he slept through the night and woke up again.

He also said: "Don't go out at night too much—that's when the bad spirits are about. If there's anything to eat, like nice fruit or any kind of meat, just put it out there and say, 'That's for you good spirits' and say, 'I want this—a nice day' or make some other request. Break off a chunk of bread and place it out for them. And in the morning take a cup of water. Drink that water—because God has given you that cleansing water for you to drink. Just take a cup and thank the Great Spirit for the day—then pray for the day. And then when you lay down, thank the Great Spirit for the day he has given you." My father did this, so I try to do that too.

Short Bull, or possibly Little Warrior.

One time my husband had to stay home while I took Georgie and Regina up to the Custer celebration of Gold Discovery Days.[10] Leo was working then for Albert Yankton, putting up hay. So my husband would stay here at home all by himself—sleeping here at night and going to help Albert in the morning. They always helped each other.

Anyway, he came home one evening, and it was still light outside. It wasn't quite dark. Leo was coming down the hill toward the house, and he could hear my father singing icilowan [death song] in the house. He tied up his horse,

*walked in, and knew he was present in there. Leo said out
loud: "I hear your voice, but I hope nothing bad happens in
our family." So then he said some prayers and went to bed.*

*Now my father was alive at this time, but he was at the
Sioux San Hospital in Rapid City. Also in that hospital was
my nephew, Benjamin Junior. It was just a short time after
Leo heard my father singing that Benjamin Junior died of
meningitis—so we knew my father was preparing us for it.*

▼

chapter nine

▼

Farewell

Black Elk knew that life's circle was nearly complete, and he calmly awaited his passing. In assuring Lucy that he was prepared, the holy man reported the presence of a phantom visitor that was seen only by him. This claim did not meet with disbelief on the part of his family. Lucy remembered:

One day, my father called my husband and I in and talked to us. He said that his days were coming to an end, and he told my husband, "Take care of my daughter as a father and mother would take care of her." And my husband has done that I guess. My father said, "I am old, so don't take my death too hard. Do not mourn a long time, you know I will be happy. My sufferings will be over, and I will have no hurt. Pray for me as I taught you to pray in your early days. And pray for me. Do not let any single day pass without praying for me." So the last prayer I always say before I go to bed is, "May the souls of all the faithful departed rest in peace." I say that for my father and for all who have died.

As he waited for death, he told me, "Do not worry, there is a man who comes to see me everyday at three o'clock. He is from overseas, and he comes in to pray with me—so I pray with him. He is a sacred man." When he was living, my father always used the phrase wicasa wakan *when speaking about a Blackrobe priest. And that's the phrase he used in talking about that visitor—wicasa wakan. So he might have been a Blackrobe who visited him. During this time he received his last rites for the fourth and last time.*

He told me: "I know I have a lot of little angels up there in heaven watching over me, and one day I'll see them." He said that during his life as a catechist he baptized a lot of little babies who were dying; since the priest wasn't there, he had to baptize them. Those were the ones he meant. He said that they were his "little helpers" and "guides."

He also said, "It seems like I will go anytime now, so if your car is alright, go after your younger brother. I want to see him." My brother Nick Junior was working way out about fifteen miles from Hay Springs, Nebraska, so we went to get him. He got his pay and came back, but my father died just before he returned. He passed away at my Brother Ben's house on the seventeenth of August, 1950. And he was patient with his suffering right up until the end.

When he was a catechist, he had been given a black shirt, but we couldn't lay him out in that because it was all eaten by mice. So we laid him out in a suit and tie and put his big cross around his neck. The catechists had been given those large crucifixes. He also had his big rosary—one that had big beads and a saint's relic on it. When he was out east, a bishop in New York had given him that rosary and the relic of St. Peter.

According to traditional Lakota belief, one's spirit parted the body at death and, if judged worthy, embarked upon the Milky Way, or "spirit trail," toward the "land of many lodges" (Powers 1975:191). If found wanting for some reason, it became a "wandering spirit" and was sentenced to roaming the earth until deemed fit for entrance to the better life (Hassrick 1964:297). The uncanny luminescence of the sky during Black Elk's wake was an appropriately mysterious occurrence seen as honoring the man whose spiritual vision was now entrusted to those he left behind.

During the night of his wake, natural phenomena conspired to produce images in the sky, which people interpreted as being of supernatural origin. The figures Lucy and others claim to have seen (i.e., the number 8 and a circle) might be construed in various ways. Among the Lakota, the circle was rich in symbolism, and Tyon spelled this out for Walker (1917:160):

The Oglala believe the circle to be sacred because the Great Spirit caused everything in nature to be round except stone. . . . Everything that breathes is round like the body of a man. Everything that grows from the ground is round like the stem of a tree. . . . It is also the symbol of the circle that marks the edge of the world and therefore of the four winds that travel there. . . . it is also the symbol of these divisions of time and hence the symbol of all time.

For these reasons the Oglala make their tipis circular, their camp circle circular, and sit in a circle in all ceremonies. The circle is also the symbol of the tipi and of shelter. If one makes a circle for an ornament and it is not divided in any way, it should be understood as the symbol of the world and of time.

Apropos to the occasion, Westerners might identify the figure 8 as a symbol for infinity. However, such an association is not a traditional one among the Lakota. Nonetheless, apart from being the conjunction of two circles, the figure might also be a kind of celestial marker of the month August, in which Black Elk died (an association perhaps made at the time but now forgotten). Lucy herself was unable to attach a particular meaning to the sight, the details of which are variously reported in the following narratives.[1]

Also contained in these recollections are some clarifications regarding Black Elk's birth. That is, Neihardt reported the holy man to have been born "in the Moon of the Popping Trees (December)" in 1863 (*BES*, 6), while Brown had said Black Elk was born in 1862.[2] Father Lindebner listed 1866 in the Holy Rosary Mission Archives, which was the year in which Lucy understood him to be born. She disputed the month December, saying that July was the real month of his birth and that her father had actually reported to Neihardt the date of his spiritual birth (i.e., his December baptism). Neither Ben nor Neihardt, it seems, were aware of this deeper meaning.

Throughout Black Elk's life, natural phenomena were repeatedly perceived as affirming his prayerful entreaties. Death, it seems, did not curtail this pattern; like a proclamation, a sort of galactic testimony was seen by people at Black Elk's wake. This heavenly display was understood as the sky gleaming bright to light his way to the peaceful land of many lodges.

Black Elk knew the old ways more intimately than most and confronted the transition to twentieth-century life in a manner that helped buoy others who languished. He enjoined his people not to lose their religious integrity and manifested what this responsibility entailed in the face of discouraging trends. Those present at his funeral powerfully felt a cosmic affirmation of the holy man's life and understood this sacred occurrence to be a last blessing bestowed by Wakan Tanka, through Black Elk, upon all in attendance. Lucy recollected:

The night of his wake was one I'll never forget. Others saw it that night, but they don't seem to talk about it. My father said toward the end that "I have a feeling that when I die, some sign will be seen. Maybe God will show something. He will be merciful to me and have something shown which will tell of his mercy."

What we saw that night was the sky in a way we never saw before. The northern lights were brighter than ever, and we saw those figures—the number 8 and a ring, or circle. They were separated by a short distance, but they were there—an 8 and a circle. I always wondered what that meant.

William Siehr, a Jesuit brother at Holy Rosary Mission since 1938, knew Black Elk and had attended the holy man's wake. His recollection of the night was vivid.

Well yes, I remember old Nick, he was the medicine man Neihardt talks about in Black Elk Speaks. *He was also a zealous catechist from Manderson. He had quite a bit of influence with the people, old Nick did. He was the old medicine man who, in the old days, was considered something like our priesthood. That is, they respected him for the authority he had, especially in religious matters. He was considered to be quite a noted man among the tribe.*

Anyway, I was with Father Zimmerman that night, and we went over to the wake. It was in the old house that's still standing there as you approach Manderson. There were many people sitting nearby the coffin, like they do at all the wakes, but this was a large assembly. There wasn't so much auto traffic in those days, but there were quite a few cars around, and it was impressive to see so many people there. We stayed there and spoke to many of the mourners, and it must have been around 10:30 when we started back up to the old Manderson road.

When we left the place, we noticed that light. The sky was just one bright illumination. I never saw anything so magnificent. I've seen a number of flashes of the northern lights here in the early days, but I never saw anything quite so intense as it was that night.

When we came back from the wake, the sky was lit up, and you could see those flames going into midair. It was something like a light being played on a fountain which sprays up. It seemed like it was rising and moving. There would be some flames going at a great distance way up into the sky above us. And others would be rising and coming into various groups and then, all of a sudden, spurt off on this side and then another side and then off to the center again. It was almost like day when we returned.

Everything was constantly moving. As I said, it was something like a display on a fountain of water where you see light reflecting on the water as it's being sprayed up. That's the way the sky was illumined—something like that—but it was all in every direction. That is, it was all coming up from the east and the south, the north and the west. And they'd all converge up to the top where they'd meet—rising up into the sky, and it was a tremendous sight.

They weren't stars or meteors, but rather, well, they were beams or flashes. And there was a variation of color effect in there—the whole horizon seemed to be ablaze. That's the first time and the only time I ever saw anything like it.

There were different formations in the sky that night which, to me, looked like spires, like tremendous points going up—then flashes. And it seemed like they were almost like fireworks in between. It was something like when a flare goes off in the sky—some sparkle here and there, but spread over such a vast area. And it was not just momentary. We all seemed to wonder at the immensity of it.

I don't recall just what anybody else said, but I know it was something I'll never forget. It was something I rather associated with the old man as he was buried at his funeral. Some sort of heavenly display, a celestial presentation—that's the way I looked at it. It was sort of a celebration. Old Nick had gone to his reward and left some sort of sign to the rest of us. With the Indians here, it seemed like it

John Lone Goose at the Rushville Nursing Home, 1974.

*had a real significance. I think it was symbolic. There was
something there.*[3]

During a 1979 interview, Joseph Epes Brown was asked
if he had been present at Black Elk's death (1979:63). Re-
sponding that he had been in Europe at the time, Brown did
recall what the holy man had foretold, namely, "You will
know when I am dying, because there will be a great display of some sort in the sky." Brown said this prophecy was
true because, "in talking with people on the Pine Ridge
Reservation," he was told that "the sky was filled with falling stars" when Black Elk died—"a very unusual display."
John Lone Goose reflected on that night.

*Yes, I remember that night very well, and those bright stars.
Everything looked miraclelike. I'm not the only one who
saw it. Lots of people did. They were kind of afraid, and I
was scared a little bit—but I knew it was God's will. I know*

The headstone at Black Elk's grave.

God sent those beautiful objects to shine on that old missionary. Maybe the Holy Spirit shined upon him because he was such a holy man.

The night was still and warm with nothing fearsome about it—just quiet and nice. God was with us that time. Other people said, "God is sending those lights to shine on that beautiful man." And that's what I believe.[4]

According to Lucy, Black Elk "used to say that he was born when the cherries were ripe [July], and the summer before he died he told me he would be eighty-four that year. So, he wasn't over ninety. They never used to celebrate birthdays as we do now, so he used his baptismal date as his birthday—December sixth. He did that because he would say 'I was reborn in baptism.'"

With Black Elk's passing, the reservation knew that a very special member of its community was no longer present. The holy man who had lived so well through so much had been a beacon for others struggling to make their way down the sometimes gloomy corridor of twentieth-century life. But now he was gone, and with his departure, it would seem that part of the reservation conscience had been laid to rest.

Black Elk understood his role as a Catholic catechist to be the desire of Wakan Tanka, "who had chosen him for this work," and he adopted this new form of religious expression with great zeal. The old medicine man-turned-catechist appreciated his earlier tradition but adapted to a historical ethos that made his religious quest a response to Wakan Tanka in the changing circumstances of the here and now. Such was the spiritual impression he tried to etch upon the hearts of his listeners, and Lucy was saddened to think her father's life-message had been lost.

After my father passed away, memories of him stayed with us a long time. Sometimes in church or sometimes at a gathering, somebody would get up and mention his name and speak about him. People would feel he was present in our chapel or meetinghouse. Younger people would even say that we should follow his example, support the church, and pray more often. And some people would say that when they came to church, they thought they saw my father.

Before my brother Nick died, I believe he was trying to follow in my father's footsteps. Sometimes he would pray in times of need, at social gatherings, or at funerals. He also preached and liked to sing in the choir. But his life was cut short, as I have said, when he died in 1959.

Although I don't speak of this, often we still experience my father's help in our lives. If something is going to go bad in our family, or if something is wrong, I know about it. And I think my father is responsible for this.

Just lately, when they took my boy to the hospital, I cried. We had plans for my brother Ben's memorial feast, and here my son was close to death. I asked my husband what we should do and if we should go through with the dinner. He said it was up to me. All of a sudden, something came to me like a flash—like somebody speaking to me clearly. I was told to go through with everything. So I did. What I thought was this. People would come to the memorial for something good. They would pray for the church and express their feelings about our religion—which I'm sure my father enjoyed. That's what he did when he was alive. And he would have thought as I did—to go through with the memorial. What came to mind was the time he had two coffins in church and still preached, even though those two coffins held his own children. I know my father was speaking to me then. We experience things like that.

My son really made a mistake when he went through that sweatlodge ceremony, thinking it was his grandfather's wish. He went and did it, got sick, and almost died. Just before he was flown to the Denver hospital, Georgie was given the last rites and communion. His mouth was dry, so he couldn't swallow the communion and had it on his tongue the entire trip. When he arrived, he got water and could swallow. My son recovered after a long stay there. He said many bad spirits came to fight him, but there was always one good spirit—Jesus. And the bad couldn't do anything to him. That was a miracle.

So when things aren't going right, I remember what my father used to say. "At such times," he would say, "go to church. It is a place of comfort where you will not feel bad.

There's a quiet peace in there. There are no quarrels and
nothing is wrong in that church.

"We Indians originally had a wanagi tipi [spirit lodge].
When a family member died, a piece of their hair would be
cut off and hung in the back of a tepee. A pipe would be
there too.[5] *If it's their child, the father and mother taught*
the other children not to say anything bad in that tepee—
because it was a special place, a sacred place, a place of
prayer.

"They'd want their child to have a good life in the other
world. They wanted that one to have an easy afterlife, so
they prayed for the dead like we do now. The church is
wanagi tipi in which Our Lord is present.

"When you go in there, have no feelings of hardship, no
wrong feelings, no hatred—nothing like that. Go in there to
the Great Spirit. That's the only place where you will be
content. If you go to church, worldly things would not dis-
turb you."

So I do as he said and believe what he told me. Some-
times I offer Holy Communion for those who don't do us
wrong, and I pray for those who have done us wrong. In
that way, I get back on the road again. I know my father led
a life like that, and I'm sure he prays for me in the other
world. He prays, as do all the poor souls, for us who are
living all confused.

A while back, somebody came and reported that certain
people were saying bad things about me. When this was
told to me I thought, "They hurt me—why don't I hurt them
back?" But right away I remembered my father and all that
he taught me. When he became a catechist, he had the
same kind of trouble. But he was a patient and forgiving
man.

When I was tempted to strike back, I thought about my
father. I chose instead to follow his way. He practiced a
Christian life, and that's the faith I wanted to practice. This
younger generation is trying to live without the Christian

life. They don't seem to be interested and practice the faith.
They've been suffering, I know that. I feel bad about this at
times. So I go to my room, like my father, and pray for
them. I pray that one day they'll return and do as they're
supposed to do—fear God according to the commandments.
I say that prayer for priests, and for unborn children being
killed.

Like her father, Lucy was discouraged in seeing relatives
and friends become lax in their practice of religion. Such
laxity, she felt, was a major reason why the social conditions of Pine Ridge were not good. In fact, Lucy saw her
own family as a microcosm of the spiritual ferment that
characterized the reservation as a whole. Some people clung
to their religious practice, and some participated halfheart-
edly. Others, meanwhile, simply seemed preoccupied with
material concerns. A sense of personal and communal mission, grounded in religion, had been lost.

This development has been a source of considerable pain
for Black Elk's daughter, and her sadness was particularly
apparent whenever our visiting would be interrupted by
happenings beyond our control. One time, for example, a
distant relative stopped by Lucy's house after a day at the
pub. Unsteady on his feet, the man was distressed to the
point of tears. Unintentionally stepping on my tape re-
corder, he held me and repeatedly implored: "Help me!"
Unmoved herself, but noticing my own uncertainty as to
what exactly I should do, Lucy calmly said, "He wants you
to pray for him."

On another occasion, I spent an afternoon with Lucy in
the presence of a relative who the previous night had been
pushed around and bruised by some neighbors. The relative laid in bed just a few feet away from us during the
course of my visit. With gun in hand, he expressed a hope
that the neighbors would stop by—so that he could shoot
them! Although greatly distracting me, the man's condi-

Ben Marrowbone in front of his house, 1977.

tion moved Lucy to state her convictions with even more force.

Because Pine Ridge was violently polarized during and after the Wounded Knee occupation of 1973, Lucy felt an even more acute need to have her father's life story told completely. A current within the reservation milieu was an invocation of Black Elk's spirit as portrayed in *Black Elk Speaks,* along with an ignoring of the Black Elk of subsequent years, or the person Lucy knew as father. She felt that people, including members of the extended family, were sorely suffering from an ignorance of Black Elk's actual life-style and thinking. Her already long-standing desire to complete his biography was fanned by the flames of a social unrest she wanted to assuage.[6]

As has been clear throughout her narrative, Lucy's devotion to the Catholic tradition of her father was ardent.

Hoping that her father's work for the church would not be forgotten, and revealing a discouragement that was perhaps similar to what he felt in later life, Lucy concluded her recollections:

The past couple of years I've been shocked to hear people say that my father never actually believed in the Catholic religion. I know they're really making a mistake. So please pray that they won't spoil my father's past life and destroy his work for the church. It's really pitiful for our younger people to believe such things and have such misunderstandings about our people. Our older people came to believe in the faith. But these days I'm asked to talk about my father's older practice, and how he rejected Christianity. If I made up stories to please people, I'd be lying. And I don't want to do that. It's not what he would have wanted.

Of historical note in the final narrative below is a reference to Calico, Ben Marrowbone's uncle, who had been a prominent figure in the early reservation community. He had been an *itancan*, or "leader." On the reservation today, a small community north of Holy Rosary Mission is named Calico, after him. Tapisleca (spleen) was its original name. Ben Marrowbone offers these final reflections.

Saving your soul was important to us. That's why the Indian used to keep a relic of someone who died. It would be kept in a tepee maybe two years or four years. This was called a wanagi tipi, or "spirit lodge." My uncle Calico had a daughter for four years, a nice girl, but she died. He kept some of her hair as a relic.

People had to show respect for the spirit of the person who died. That relic would be kept in the tepee, and no sharp words were to be spoken in its presence. No quarreling or even loud talk was to be done in that house—because there was a spirit in there. So people respected the dead, and prayed for them. If children forgot and were noisy, or if they went into the tepee before a visitor entered, they would be scolded. Visitors might come and show respect for the relic of the dead. And if little children did not show respect for the visitors, they would afterward be told: "You are impolite . . . you have no manners."

Visiting the church was like visiting the wanagi tipi. Care for the soul and praying for the dead were not new things to us. As I said, when men like Black Elk converted, nobody said, "You fool!" My father's special friend was a screech owl, and he cured people with the screech owl's help. But when my father started to change his ways to church ways, no more screech owl. He changed his practice.

▼

chapter ten

▼

Evaluations

Kiowa scholar N. Scott Momaday has written that in *Black Elk Speaks* "we have access to a principal world view of one of the major tribes of American Indians . . . without knowing precisely where to place [the book] in our traditional categories of learning" (1984:81). Appropriately, he continues, it has been used in such disciplines as literature, anthropology, folklore, religious studies, and Native American studies. Momaday further adds that "we need not concern ourselves with labels here, any more than we need concern ourselves with the question of authorship or the quality of translation or transcription." Rather, Momaday urges us simply to recognize the book as "an extraordinary human document . . . the record of a profoundly spiritual journey, the pilgrimage of a people towards their historical fulfillment and culmination, towards the accomplishment of a worthy destiny" (31).

Momaday could have said more if the preceding chapters had been accessible to analysis. They show that the Lakota own a broader sense of self-definition than what has been popularly portrayed, and that Black Elk's "profoundly spiritual journey" entailed more than was previously revealed. Until now, the people's pilgrimage included paths not clearly charted, and this omission has significantly tailored perceptions concerning Lakota adaptation to change.

In *Black Elk Speaks* and *The Sacred Pipe,* the holy man's life addressed a broad spectrum of human concerns, and many people from around the world paid special attention to what he had to say. This widespread response suggests that his books offered something more than just an interesting study of a man's thought. Black Elk himself alluded to this "more" when he described a sacred ritual to Brown and reflected on the meaning and purpose of life itself. He tearfully observed that "some [were] not even trying to catch it" (1953:138). Momaday said that such a focus was foremost in Black Elk's thought and was essentially what constituted his appeal. Regardless of its philosophical implications, however, his life story has needed a complete telling that might make the previous work more understandable to readers far removed from an earlier Lakota milieu.

In *Black Elk Speaks,* the world received a biography that gave birth to many reprints and innumerable footnotes of opinion and commentary.[1] For the most part, Neihardt's work was read as symbolizing the life journey of the Sioux and, by extension, Native people as a whole. As the preceding chapters have shown, however, more could have been added.

This fuller portrait was sketched by persons who were closest to Black Elk. Their addition provides, as carefully as possible, a better sense of the issues and individuals who composed the cultural horizon of the postreservation period within which Black Elk and his people confronted change. A more holistic portrayal, it lengthens the script of a human drama that initially captured audiences with details that were incomplete.

As shown, Black Elk attained luminary status over the

past several decades among reading audiences as a whole, and among Native people in particular. The general public tended to revere him as an eminently praiseworthy nineteenth-century figure, and social scientists pretty much regarded his life and thought as distillations of a Plains Indian culture that is no more (Hoover 1979). His books were tapped for purposes of cross-cultural comparison and were regarded as a fairly good ethnographic index to Lakota ways of the century past.

Many readers of the Black Elk canon were gripped emotionally. They saw that conquest by whites dealt death to an entire way of life, and the holy man's moving reflections conjured up a powerful vision of those better, yet bygone, days. His compelling observations painted a portrait of extinction for the once-nomadic and proud Lakota people, who now were confined and lifeless. However, his completed biography begs a reexamination of previous material that has figured so prominently within the forging of contemporary Native identity.[2]

Because religion has played an important role within the Indian revitalization movement, Black Elk's vigorous Catholic practice might perhaps stir the most controversy. It runs contrary to what Deloria outlined in *God Is Red,* a text that rode the crest of revivalism largely because of its articulate dismissal of Christianity's relevance for Indian people. A respected social critic and a Lakota himself, Deloria wrote that in Native religion "there is no demand for a personal relationship with a personal savior. Cultural heroes are representative of community experience. They may stand as classic figures, such as Deganiwidah, Sweet Medicine, Black Elk, Smohalla, and even Wovoka" (1973:201). Black Elk's completed biography, however, shows that today's emphasis on "returning to the ways of our grandfathers" can run the risk of replicating moviedom's tendency toward romantic portrayals. A popular sentiment is tapped, but it may be more imaginative than real in reflecting what transpired a century past within the hearts and minds and struggles of the senior generation.[3] Since "grandfather's ways" were more of a search than a well-established discovery, advocates of a "return" might find themselves embracing what their forebears chose to relinquish, modify, or regard as nonessential.

Deloria also stated that "more than one Indian political organization has based its approach to modern problems on *Black Elk Speaks* (1973:51)." He further suggested the book captured what was authentically Indian. Now, however, Black Elk's last sixty years offer a more nuanced perspective on the earlier work, and some may find this later period tainted through "guilt by association" with Western ways (as Brown had said). It was during this "tainted" period, however, that the holy man's inspirational thought was recorded for posterity.

The task then remains to discern what is consistent in Black Elk's life despite the apparently conflicting portrayals. Contemporary social trends might resurrect as sacrosanct a nineteenth-century Indian identity, with the Black Elk model reigning as a favorite, but the biographies should be appraised in their totality. The derivative sketch is far more satisfying, if for no other reason than its completeness.

Framing the problem this way, a significant qualification has been put forth. The man presented here is not a disconsolate elder mourning the loss of a past forever gone. Nor is he a type of Indian "Dick the bootblack," an artificer of some new Native American dream à la Horatio Alger.

Black Elk's adult life has special merit in that it calls for a reevaluation of long-held notions concerning the adaptation of Lakota people to changing times. As indicated, Plains warrior society was itself a relatively short-lived phenomenon. And yet, a static concept of Indianness, wedded only to the nineteenth-century world, has often entrenched itself, for laypeople at least, as the beginning and end of discourse related to Native identity.

Two Leggings of the Crow, interviewed shortly before his death in 1923, epitomizes the orthodoxy that has been too readily accepted as diagnostic of the Indian world at large. Having recounted his life experiences up to 1888, Two Leggings sadly concluded: "Nothing happened after that. We just lived. There were no more war parties, no capturing of horses from the Piegans and the Sioux, no buffalo to hunt. There is nothing more to tell" (Nabokov 1967:197).

Before he died in 1932, Plenty Coups, another Crow leader, reported much the same: "When the buffalo went away the hearts of my people fell to the ground, and they could not lift them up again. After this nothing happened" (Linderman 1962:311).

While Neihardt was interviewing Black Elk, Robert Gessner tapped a similar sentiment within one of his Lakota consultants. "After Wounded Knee all ambition was taken out of us. We have never since been able to regain a foothold" (1931:417).

Such accounts poignantly tell of the cataclysmic social upheaval that Indian groups endured. They report the incalculable toll in lives and lifeways that occurred within Native America and make a euphemism out of academic writings that describe the historic period as simply a "transitional phase of culture." The accent of this literature is grim and compelling, but it errs by being overly retrospective and fatalistic—at least from the updated Black Elk's point of view. Furthermore, defining Indian resilience as little more than a museum piece overlooks the ongoing struggle of Native people in the modern world.

Lucy was largely unaware of the international interest generated by her father's life story, but she was quite attuned to local concerns. She sought to change the image of her father that younger people were beginning to construct, and she wanted known the entirety of what Black Elk spoke. Latter-day revisionists could do what they wanted with her father's books, but Lucy considered herself to be the primary source for defining where further discussion would lead. Lakota sources confirmed the account she gave, so her familial perspective was validated by the community who knew him most intimately.

Traditional Lakota identity had been ascribed to a man who lived most of his life in the twentieth century, but the greater part of his life was never reported. As legitimate as a study of his younger days might have been, it went only so far, and Lucy sought to flesh out a portrait that was heretofore incomplete. As a result, an important by-product of her effort and that of others has been to show how Lakota, before and after their reservation experience, adjusted to changing conditions.

With Black Elk's life bridging significantly distinct periods, a diachronic perspective emerges that few, if any, biographies have provided. It reveals the old culture as an adaptive one, and the holy man as typifying its essence; that is, he was flexible and responsive to the demands of changing conditions. He was neither an artifactual relic of the bison-hunting era, nor was he a prisoner to its substance, even though much literature and opinion suggest this was the case—for him and most others.

DeMallie pointed out that the previous work on Black Elk deserves criticism precisely because of its depiction of him "as more aloof and cut-off from the real world than he actually was" (1984a:124). This is an understatement that has far-reaching implications. Notably, the Black Elk model of Lakota identity has been sustained by both scholarly opinion and Native self-perception to the detriment of, among other things, his people's present-day social adjustment.

Although noted in earlier descriptions of reservation life (MacGregor 1946:26-27), the Lakota desire for a return to what is imagined as a more carefree and pristine condition has emerged with even greater force in recent years. With their sociocultural horizon limited to the more dramatic events of historical times, writers have expended much effort depicting Black Elk's people as a "warrior society" during that zenith period. It is convincingly argued that pursuing military exploits was fundamental to their corporate identity (Hyde 1937; MacGregor 1946; Hassrick 1964; Anderson 1984).

Studies that describe the anomic conditions of twentieth-century reservation life intimate that the Lakota have been disenfranchised from a most important pursuit (i.e., military adventure). Students of Indian culture then perceive the modern era as filled with sad people who mourn their inability to raise war parties or to "count coup" (and wear the associated feathers). Presumably, the social institutions of the past drew their lifeblood from this central activity, and with it gone, the Lakota are reduced to a lingering depression, a grueling and tortuous assimilation, or perhaps (many hope) a new cultural synthesis somehow congruent with a more "glorious" past.

Most of the literature (and folk opinion) has used this terminology either directly or indirectly when referring to Black Elk's people. (It is a warrior astride his mount in the famous *End of the Trail* sculpture.) A review of Lakota culture, however, shows that "warrior society" (and the associations it evokes) is misleading. Now reduced to a commonly shared vernacular, the designation seems explanatory but is not, in fact, as illuminating as it suggests.[4] An undue emphasis has prevailed that the Black Elk biography tempers.

The Lakota ascent to what has been called their Plains dominance was actually a hard-fought and continuous negotiation (Little Thunder n.d.). That is, the Crow, Kiowa, and other groups did not passively submit to being displaced. Rather, they fought to retain their own foothold within a buffalo-bounded ecosystem. During this process, American expansion accentuated militancy and brought prominence to such Lakota leaders as Crazy Horse, Red Cloud, and Sitting Bull. These figures surface as representatives of a long, ongoing struggle for existence that characterized the historical period. The phrase "warrior society" accurately labels an obvious aspect of Plains culture, but it does not reflect the overall systemic adaptation of the people. The economic sphere lends support to this perspective, as the short period of successful, early-reservation pastoralism is a significant indication of the Lakota willingness to forsake a contingency life-style in favor of a more predictable, less-trying mode.

Did Black Elk speak on behalf of a warrior society? Neihardt's interview material contained more militant overtones than appeared in the finished text, but these omissions did not substantially alter a sense of the nineteenth-century milieu that he described. The period was, simply, one of immense struggle marked by the violence of war. Ultimately, then, the explicative value of "warrior society" is minimal, and its relevance to contemporary Lakota can only be metaphoric, as in speaking of the people's "fight" for social justice. Two-thirds of Black Elk's life, like that of many others from his generation, was clearly a decision for alternative routes to survival.

Ethnographic evidence presents a picture quite different from the one so often portrayed by modern media or war buffs. As much as Ruth Hill's best-seller *Hanta Yo* (1979) was criticized, it at least showed how lifeways of the nineteenth-century *gradually* came to be. The Lakota did not just one day decide that social status would be commensurate with coup counts. Sex roles did not become fixed so as to assure success in battle, and nomadism was not imperative because of a newfound equine "technology." Terminology of this nature has tended to distance readers from the actual minds and hearts of Lakota individuals who struggled to survive. The prereservation period was not, in short, free of duress. Maintaining existence via regular war parties was a cultural value that the people would relinquish willingly, should survival be negotiated by other means.

A rereading of the historical period might indeed reveal that war was a way of life, but only because the Lakota were of necessity a defense-minded people (a characteristic noted even in recent years). However, they also occupied themselves with other activities. Their defensiveness was initially not by design but because of pressure exerted upon them by other Native groups. Rather than making a preferential option for war and a military regimen, the people were simply wise enough to protect a long-sought territorial niche.

Far from being a well-oiled military machine, Lakota society maintained a posture sufficient for boundary maintenance. War exploits never required mobilization of very great numbers and in fact seem to have equaled as much or as little time spent on other activities (Two Bulls n.d.). The much-publicized victory of Little Big Horn in 1876 was a grand exception to the rule (over many years) of relatively inconsequential battles. Therefore, instead of considering the warrior element of Lakota society as somehow its essential attribute, it might better be understood as defensive in nature and as but one means of gaining social status—a cultural category subject to fluctuation and variety (One Feather n.d.). Stated in simpler terms, the taking up of arms was a necessity for the protection of kith and kin. Nonetheless, portrayal of the Lakota as an inherently hostile people no doubt lingers because of other reasons only alluded to until now.

Primarily, the United States still fought this "enemy" as recently as 1891. Shortly after this final clash, the advent of the film industry captivated the world and capitalized on America's recently defeated "savage" foes. Ever since, westerns have reinforced the tried-and-true box office draw of Sioux adversaries stalking innocent, yet brave, settlers. Such celluloid fare, and the plethora of Zane Grey or Louis L'Amour-like novels, no doubt greatly influences our national perception. Their repetitive imaging of Native people has created, both inside the classroom and out, a cultural stereotype that Indians themselves find easy to accept.

An example of how perception and reality can conflict in this regard might be seen in the Wounded Knee occupation of 1973. Occurring in the bitter cold of winter, deadly to some of its participants, and divisive of the community, the event was a severely painful experience for the reservation as a whole. Support for the occupation came from an assortment of Native people and sympathetic non-Indians because of anger and frustration arising from grievances that always seemed to go unheeded. What it measurably accomplished is difficult to say, but it has become synonymous with heroic resistance from times past (Akwesasne Notes 1974), and people present at the occupation command a certain reverence for being Wounded Knee "warriors." Fertile imaginations, after the fact, seem to have constructed a reality quite different from the original.[5]

Concurrent with Wounded Knee and its aftermath was the cult-film series featuring Billy Jack, a character who was the quintessential embodiment of an idealized warrior. The series portrayed Billy, who was an Indian, as a former Green Beret with Vietnam experience. He dispatched unfriendly whites with lethal karate kicks (an exotic martial craft apropos of exotic Indian people, so filmmakers would have audiences believe). Lakota youths and others were much entranced by the Billy Jack image; imitations of his black, brimless, beaded hat became the fashion of the day on reservations nationwide. With Billy Jack, the motion picture industry no doubt converted many viewers to the opinion that any other role model connoted a kind of genetic sellout for Indian people.[6]

The deeper truth, however, is that for over two hundred years the Lakota have had to defend themselves. In addition, one hundred years of reservation life have fostered different forms of antisocial behavior that arise largely from the hammerlock of poverty. Such responses have little to do with any kind of earlier ingrained and supposedly warrior tradition.[7]

Erik Erikson worked among the Lakota during the 1930s and addressed some of the issues raised here. He grimly reflected (correctly or not) that even if the Lakota could return to the past, their traumatic defeat and dependence would never be erased. The "psychological effects of unemployment and neurosis . . . tuberculosis, syphilis, and alcoholism" were, among other things, exacerbated when he visited them again in 1950 (1963:163). His prognosis was not very hopeful, and subsequent studies amplified the ominous forecast. They reported that children see their fathers as ineffective models, suffer from family disruption, turn to delinquency, and carry a "generalized rejection of life" (Seward 1956:230). Educational achievement was also found to be radically below that of other groups (Bryde 1966). Despite this bleak pattern, however, the Lakota remain determined to prevent it from continuing. Reservation leadership has not been blind to these issues, which itself is evidence for persons like Black Elk still playing key roles among the people.

A means proposed for the amelioration of Indian cultures in general, and Lakota culture in particular, has been a return to "tradition." Looking back at what was may seem easier to do than solving sociologically what is, but such a focus clearly does not remove all difficulties.[8] As Black Elk's life story has shown, traditions come in different forms, change over time, and compete with one another for ascendancy. His completed biography is thus an important addition to American Indian ethnohistory, since it carries discussion well beyond the staid depiction of stereotypes associated with vanquished, victimized, and "vanishing" peoples.

Langness (1965) has argued that the use of biography has not been plumbed sufficiently by anthropologists, especially since it offers a key to cultural identity that other research fails to articulate. With this comment in mind, the account here can contribute to the development of a more authentic and personalistic understanding of traditional and contemporary culture. Black Elk's completed story challenges the perhaps too facile, even though descriptive, labels and images of Indian people or the Lakota milieu (e.g., warrior society, maladaptive, acculturation, retreatism, anomie). His passage from medicine man to catechist, from horseback to motorcycle and cars, from forager to successful rancher, from buffalo subsistence to sauerkraut, and from buckskin to three-piece suits provides a more accurate picture of what it has meant, and does mean, to be a Lakota. Just as his people owned a broader definition than commonly assumed, so did Black Elk's life include all this, and more.

The special commemorative edition of *Black Elk Speaks* featured an introduction that, because of the omission of this fuller account, reinforced a theoretical misdirection that now might be amended. Namely, the author noted how Neihardt's work had "become a North American bible of all tribes" (Deloria 1979:xiii) and contended that it must be considered an essential canon of Native spirituality from which further theological reflection ought to arise. He said that the book's unanticipated popularity was what Black Elk would have wanted, and that it could serve as an alternative to Western religious thought.

Aware of its authorship problems, Deloria nonetheless gave the work his blessing because of the "transcendent truth" it spoke to all people. Also, a more congenial, culturally rooted religion could be tapped within the life story, since Black Elk represented a kind of lost legacy of religious strength.[9] Culture contact had dispossessed Indian people of everything they had formerly cherished, but Black Elk somehow had stood firm in his beliefs. Despite this popular characterization of the book (and *The Sacred Pipe*), critics have argued that the theology articulated was Neihardt's, not Black Elk's (Holler 1984b:20). When scholars adopt such contrary positions, it is difficult to determine exactly what this holy man of the earlier works actually thought.

The completed biography constitutes an addendum that clarifies these disparate types of observation. Black Elk's life prescription, if it can be so labeled, was not a call for the restoration of traditional Native rites; nor was his Christian practice a signal for renewed evangelistic endeavors among Native peoples for the sake of eradicating an older tradition's religious forms. By the same token, Christianity's importance within the holy man's life cannot be underestimated. His legacy was most succinctly stated in the words of a ninety-year-old relative who appraised her cousin's behavior and thought as follows: "He was a really good fellow. He'd preach about the Gospel. He'd say to 'bring up children according to God's laws. Only Almighty God can change the way things are!' "[10] A witness to what his life had entailed, she distrusted any further reports that time would add to his memory and angrily indicted her people by saying: "Younger ones now don't tell the truth. They never believed. People heard him but did not listen." Her forthright comments were telling. So much was implied in so little.

The Wounded Knee massacre was an event of her early childhood, while her many years were passed in residence near Manderson itself. Matriarch of both the reservation and its Catholic community, this outspoken grandmother knew her cousin to be a man who had lived through many difficult times, a man who had been the district's first and foremost catechist, and one whose "family could have taken better care of him than they did." A woman whose religious instruction was clearly the same as Black Elk's, she shared his lament that the years had devastated the people's behavior. What previously had been a reflexive, spiritual perspective on life was now, in her opinion, not much in evidence among the people.

Black Elk's life clearly encourages a renewed interest in cultural roots that would enliven religious ideology and practice. Ironically, however, when this topic is broached in modern contexts, it is often framed in terms that conflict with the experience of people like Black Elk and his cousin, themselves paragons of tradition. An unidentified speaker at the 1975 Intertribal Conference held in Alberta, Canada, illustrates this paradox. "I'm not condemning that religion that the White man was given to by God. That's *his* religion. It was given to him on another island. Us, too, we was given a way to worship the Creator on this island, but we have lost parts of it, and it's up to us to find it again, and relive it, and be Indian people again." The speaker's position is reminiscent of Brown, who said that Black Elk's Christian years were seen as compromising his Indianness. Hence, Native peoples and others have earnestly struggled to make sense of historical facts (e.g., the conversion experiences), which cannot be dismissed lightly.

Aware that elders have quite openly accommodated non-Native religious traditions, revivalists repudiate the conversion phenomenon in conciliatory terms, along the lines of what another unidentified conference speaker explained: "That's the trouble with our people. When they changed, and they believed, they believed with all their hearts. Then it's hard to bring them back to the right road. But our young people realized that they weren't on the right road. And a few of our elders realized, so they are helping us to come back to the right road."

Black Elk's participation in Christianity, and that of others from his generation, is thus evaluated as sincere, but misguided. A National Geographic film even quoted "the great Oglala Sioux holy-man Black Elk" as prophesying the sentiments expressed above—sentiments that contradict precisely what Black Elk communicated to those who knew him best. Moreover, the film's narrator attributed to Black Elk a prophecy that claimed: "The fifth generation would bring back the old ways. In the fifth generation, Indian people would begin to regain strength and pride. It is now the era of the fifth generation."[11] As authoritative as the educational film may sound, or as persuasive as its arguments ultimately might be, its use of the previous Black Elk material only perpetuates a hermeneutical problem that has been so long-standing. That is, according to the stenographic record, Black Elk actually said, "Perhaps in the sixth generation the tree will bloom as in my vision" (DeMallie 1984b:265).

The interpretation of imagery that appears in this type of literature (and its application to the present) is not, however, the exact science that the film (or other sources) might offer it to be. Contrary to what it might have intended, National Geographic did not provide much clarity as the film equivalently added Black Elk's vision to a lineage of prophetic material that has included such diverse offspring as the Bible, numerology, tarot cards, Nostradamus, and astrology. The symbolic content of these forms and now the vision, the tree, and "six generations" is inherently so diffuse that interpretive difficulties abound. Nonetheless, Black Elk's words can be used to sanction ideologies not easily associated with the person my consultants knew as father and friend.

Black Elk's life and thought can be understood more readily within the context of the religious dynamics of the early reservation. Seen in this light, his portrait of zealous catechist and discouraged elder will not remain the paradoxical profile that bars understanding. That is, much of the discussion spawned by Black Elk has focused on an either-or proposition: he was, at heart, either an old-time medicine man or one who forsook the tradition in favor of something entirely new.[12] What follows will show that neither evaluation is an appropriate framing of the issue.

DeMallie has pointed out that "effective leadership for the Lakotas shifted during the early reservation period from political to religious spheres" (1984b:23).[13] It is not surprising that this change should occur. In his study of Plains Indian religion, Schwarz noted that "the holy man has a 'vision' of the world—its nature, its history and its destiny—and a sense of humanity's place within that scheme. Through that vision, the holy man can hope to solve problems for which the tradition offers no ready-made solutions" (1981:53). It should be clear why such persons were especially prominent during the late nineteenth century. The fluid nature of Plains culture itself made it conducive for religious leadership to emerge even more significantly. As shown, it was Black Elk's abiding sense of religious mission that permitted his own meaningful adaptation to changing circumstances.

A corroborating source for this same theme can be found in the person of George Sword, Walker's multidimensional consultant and man "of marked ability with a philosophical trend far beyond the average Ogalala" (1917:59). In his unfinished autobiography, Sword disclosed that:

> When I believed the Oglala Wakan Tanka was right I served him with all my powers. I became a Wicasa Wakan (holy man) . . . a pejuta wicasa (medicine man) . . . a Blotaunka (leader of war parties). . . . I was Wakiconze (civil magistrate). . . . In the war with the white people I found their Wakan Tanka the Superior . . . and have served Wakan Tanka according to the white people's manner and with all my power. . . . I joined the church and am a deacon in it and shall be until I die. I have done all I was able to do to persuade my people to live according to the teachings of the Christian ministers (159).

An Episcopalian, Sword was not unlike Black Elk and many others, who, as MacGregor pointed out, "translated Christianity into the Dakota [sic] way of life"—interpreting it in terms of their previous religious experience (1946:102). Combined with traditions that had evolved earlier, this experience included (from their most immediate past) the Ghost Dance, which was itself an import that they received and accommodated. Here, the religious lens through which the Lakota viewed existence was circumspect in that an inventory of things supernatural was open-ended. Maintaining a foothold on the Plains did not allow the luxury of parochial definitions for what was perceived as an omnipresent and awesome fact of life, the immanence and mystery of Wakan Tanka.

Equally notable at this time was Short Bull. He and Sword were prominent public figures who came to terms with both the Ghost Dance and Christianity and who, like Black Elk, verify the normative role these types of persons played as religious leaders confronting change.[14] Theirs was a challenge, as Overholt described, "to put/keep the world together, and as such was fraught with ambiguity" (1978:190–91). It should be kept in mind, however, that survival on the Plains was filled with this ambiguity long before the reservation period. Hence, the role of the holy men ought to be seen as long-standing within the tradition and not just a creation of these more recent times.

Steinmetz classified tradition and innovation as it pertained to religion under two labels: Lakota Ecumenist I and II (1980). The former refers to those who practice the old and the new traditions separately, while the latter are those who work to integrate them in some way. Disputing Black Elk's classification within the second category, Holler argued that the holy man was clearly a traditionalist for Neihardt and Brown, a dutiful Catholic while employed as a catechist (1984a:41). Steinmetz's reading of Black Elk's experience stressed an integration that was largely unconscious (1980:159), while Holler sought to establish the holy man as a proponent for the practice of traditional rites. Neither evaluation, however, takes fully into account the cultural landscape within which Black Elk lived. In this discussion, it is necessary to realize that life-style and religious practice were not distinct spheres.

The Lakota world of the late nineteenth century was characterized by upheavals that radically altered the people's manner of life. It was during this period that Black Elk was born and raised. Formative in his and the people's experience were such cultural cornerstones as the vision quest, the Sun Dance, nomadism, and the buffalo hunt. Sitting Bull's surrender in 1881, however, marked the end of the nomadic way, sealing once and for all the reservation system still in place today. The last great buffalo hunt was held the following year, and this ushered in a new economy that, ever since, has amounted to some form of subsistence based on government rationing.

Where success, power, and the virtuous life could come from Wakan Tanka through the vision quest, this avenue was gradually sealed off by a variety of measures imposed by the reservation's superintendent. Certain customs were outlawed (notably, the Sun Dance), children were made to leave home and then board at government schools (some, like Ben Black Elk, were taken to Carlisle, Pennsylvania), and sodalities that formerly flourished gradually lost their significance. In fact, reservation-born youth came into a world quite different from that of their parents. Those who rallied around the Ghost Dance of 1890 were, in all probability, the last to have experienced a vision quest that was independent of agency concern, or a Sun Dance that symbolized and reinforced group solidarity.

Witness to and participant in this unfolding drama, Black Elk embodied traditional Lakota ideology as he manifested a resilient willingness to let go of what was and to experiment with what might be the disclosures of Wakan Tanka for his life. Like others similarly situated, he traveled overseas and endured whatever unknowns such a venture entailed. Disillusioned there, he listened to reports of a messiah and, again like others, embraced the new hope offered by ghost dancing.

Where Linton would call participation in the Ghost

Dance an irrational flight from reality (1943), and where Mooney would call it a response to recent and long-standing grievances (1896), persons like Black Elk were willing adherents, owing to a well-conditioned, culturally based disposition toward seeking the power of Wakan Tanka on whatever new horizon it might appear. Earlier in life, while with the Wild West Show in England, Black Elk wrote: "All along I live remembering God. . . . [T]he show runs day and night . . . but all along I live remembering God *so he enables me to do it all.* . . . I know the White man's customs well. One custom is very good. Whoever believes in God will find good ways—that is what I mean" (DeMallie 1984b:8, italics added).

Upon returning to Pine Ridge in 1889, Black Elk again recounted his experiences and once more revealed a religious questing that was thematic to his life. "Of the White man's many customs, only his faith, the White man's beliefs about God's will, and how they act according to it, I wanted to understand. . . . So Lakota people, trust in God! Now all along I trust in God" (DeMallie 1984b:9–10). Nearly twenty years later, now working as a catechist, Black Elk echoed these same sentiments, which had guided him through so much. His letter of October 20, 1907, in *Sinasapa Wocekiye Taeyanpaha* says:

There I met with the White people in a meeting, and I was really glad that I have heard and seen with my own eyes the things they are doing. And we should do the same thing here, but it is very hard for us to do the things that the White people are doing because we have very few things to work with. But again, we must depend on God to help us. My friends and relatives I speak to you from the bottom of my heart. Please try and do the things that we're supposed to do. Let us not forget the main person—that is, Wakan Tanka.

The worldview represented here is a spiritual approach

to life in which religious thought dictates behavior. Lakota holy men like Black Elk were the more visible representatives of this process, but a comparable disposition lay within the population as a whole. Lakota society was not at a loss in surfacing and affirming religious leadership roles, which proliferated within the emerging denominations.

Linton stated that movements such as the Ghost Dance arose during the acculturative process, when exploitation and frustration are experienced by a dominated people (1943). According to Mooney's thesis, the Ghost Dance was only a symptom and expression of the real causes of dissatisfaction that had been growing among the Lakota (1896). Valid as these observations might be, they simply represent a phenomenological description of the more apparent conditions of the early reservation social milieu. Black Elk's completed biography, however, illuminates the "cognitive map" that guided people like himself *past* the Ghost Dance and into still another mode of adaptation, namely, active participation within an organized denomination of Christianity, along with the acculturation such participation included.

Like others of his generation, Black Elk had been a respected religious practitioner, and when such persons affiliated with Christian sects, their following did not turn a deaf ear on this already-established leadership. As Lucy herself stated, the missionaries seemed to look for such persons. People received the assuring presence of their own religious specialists—many of whom, it appeared, were successfully discerning a new course that seemed to have the blessing of Wakan Tanka. Regardless of affiliation, the holy men were bridges of adaptation who strove to lead the people into new regions of experience. Their fundamental role was to preserve and foster a religious consciousness that had so long enabled the people to confront whatever challenged them.[15]

Essentially, when people like Black Elk or Sword, Fills

the Pipe, or Black Fox strove to lead their people into the twentieth century, their role as new-order holy men served the people well, providing a self-direction that was elsewhere very difficult to experience. This self-direction, a kind of vision quest gone communal, explains in large part why denominational affiliations became so widespread and important during the early reservation period. External conditions could drastically change and be controlled or manipulated by non-Lakota agents, but the people's internal environment was theirs to determine.[16] Missionaries seem to have spoken a religious language that was comprehensible to the holy men. The latter, in turn, translated the new revelation to a following who trusted their discernment.

Discussion of such a process becomes fruitless when attempts are made to quantify Christian accretions or Lakota residues, and conscious or unconscious reconstructions. Theological speculation, if it can be called that, has been shown in Black Elk's life to happen as instinctive, or as a matter of course, when he spoke with priests or other catechists, or with anyone who broached the topic. Neihardt and Brown were simply the first to report, in print, the thoughts of a man whose life had long been given to such reflection. Among the more recent examples, Fools Crow's biography is additional evidence of this same pattern at work.[17]

A case has been made for viewing *The Sacred Pipe* as Black Elk's Lakota counterpoint to Catholic sacraments—a kind of compromising syncretism being the result. However, the holy man's disposition was not so narrow.[18] He did not seem to have felt "the need of coordinating and systematizing . . . beliefs as strongly as we do" (Durkheim 1965:193). The early Black Elk material might suggest this kind of analysis, but his more comprehensive portrait advises analytical restraint. That is, the holy man did not embrace Christian practices only insofar as they matched traditional constructs. Nor did his Christian perspective divorce him from the essentials of Lakota spirituality for in fact there was only one essential to maintain: namely, searching for and reliance upon Wakan Tanka in the every-day course of events.

MacGregor's sociological study of Pine Ridge provides a fruitful perspective on issues that bore upon Black Elk toward the end of his life. Importantly, his work illumi-nates the social context within which Neihardt and Brown found the holy man; that is, his research was undertaken during the years *between* visitations by the authors. Most pertinent is MacGregor's comment on religious practice. "Christian Churches too appear to be losing some of their former hold as . . . many Indians are now following the trend of the local white population away from control by the Church" (1940:103).

Residents of Pine Ridge, although removed from main-stream America, were not insulated from the secularizing forces of the dominant society. World War II contributed to this trend by drawing large numbers into the armed forces, while relocation programs similarly expanded Lakota ex-perience. Such in outline was the unfolding social scene that Black Elk witnessed. Not only did many people have a loose hold on traditional religious forms, but they were also showing laxity in their practice of the Christian or, indeed, any way.

Black Elk's reprimand in later life of the Manderson Catholic community reveals the kind of discouragement he endured as an elder. Far from being an acknowledgment of his erroneous Catholic practice, *The Sacred Pipe* was sim-ply another attempt to rally his people's religious fervor by whatever means were at his disposal. Earlier in life he re-spected the Thin Elk decision to resume traditional par-ticipation and to discontinue Christian practice—not be-cause he felt their choice was theologically more sound or because he was indifferent to their concerns or because he was vacillating in his own commitment. Important to Black

Elk was the quest itself. Whereas his destiny was that of a Catholic catechist, others might pursue alternate paths. The Thin Elk decision, because it was apparently rooted in sincerity, was a journey upon which he could bestow his blessing. By contrast, the elder Black Elk seems to have been discouraged by so many people abandoning a trek in *any* direction.

Evaluations of what actually transpired when Christianity encountered Native religious practice are sometimes puzzling, as in the case of Grobsmith's ethnography on the Rosebud Lakota. She cites, for example, the "popular notion . . . that Catholic missionaries were cruel and patronizing to the Indians" (1981:83) and suggests, via MacGregor (1946:92), that the early reservation period can be summarily regarded as a time when "missionaries created resistance by trying to eradicate the native religion instead of using it as a frame of reference in which to introduce Christianity. They attempted to impose Christian morality by suppressing Indian custom. . . . They tried to drive out indiscriminately Indian ways which had no relation to religion in the Indian mind." She admits, however, that "there is also clear evidence that the church in general and the clergy in particular devoted great efforts toward assisting the Sioux during the most harrowing period in their history." Her conclusion is that "succeeding generations made . . . their peace with Christianity" and that it is surprising "the high degree to which Christianity has been assimilated into native life . . . considering its low acceptance initially" (1981:83).

Such interpretations are difficult to understand. Maybe the abundance of catechists disproves what is assumed to be a "low acceptance" of Christianity among the people. Perhaps the popular notion about "cruel and patronizing" Catholic missionaries is mistaken, for why did succeeding generations bother to "make peace" in light of such a history?

Representatives of the different denominations no doubt

had many varied encounters with many varied individuals within diverse contexts. As Prucha has pointed out: "A variety of white settlers, agents, soldiers, and missionaries created a complex web of relationships that is almost impossible, in this latter day, to disentangle. All that one person can reasonably be expected to do is to investigate particular groups, aspects, or activities, a few at a time, with the hope that each study will contribute to a better understanding of the whole." (1988:130). This complexity is perhaps why Grobsmith cautions those who might rely too heavily on one evaluation of so complex an interaction:

History . . . will reveal the very deep if ambivalent relationship between the Indians and the church and the secure place the church occupies in most people's lives. . . . Although missionaries may have capitalized on a situation ideal for introducing a new religion, the Indian people recognized that those missionaries were not themselves to blame for the changes; on the contrary, their sympathetic assistance was deeply appreciated and still is to this day. . . . It is common for the non-Indian outsider to regard Christianity as alien to the Indian. But, in fact, nearly all Lakota are Christians, even those who are also active in native ritual. For the Indian people themselves, the church is an integral and important institution in Lakota society. (1981:82, 86)[19]

The content of the above citation is reflected in Black Elk's life. Given the paucity of such encompassing biographies as his, the non-Indian outsider, some Native people themselves, and knowledgeable others may not be aware of this broader perspective.

The previous focus on Black Elk's early Lakota formation deserves qualification because it does not adequately reflect the social system that now has been long in place among his people—a social system with which he was quite familiar. As a result, the holy man of Neihardt and Brown cannot enlighten cultural discourse in quite the same way as before. During my relationship with Lucy, however, a series of incidents occurred that tended only to reinforce the earlier, incomplete portrayal of Black Elk's life.

I was invited to attend a special picnic the family had planned. Christopher Sergel, a New York playwright, had composed a work based on *Black Elk Speaks,* and he thought it important that his lead (actor David Carradine) and entourage visit Black Elk's surviving relatives. Included with the group was John Neihardt's daughter, Hilda, who served as the expedition's photographer.

Familiar with Carradine's popular television series "Kung Fu," the younger members of the family were quite excited to be hosting such a celebrity. Their enthusiasm was contagious, since the older folk decided to slaughter a cow for this special occasion (no small thing for people who were quite destitute). Ironically, this special gesture of Lakota hospitality was not mentioned by anyone, and so their sacrifice went unnoticed by the featured guest, who, it turned out, was a practicing vegetarian.

The playwright and his wife comported themselves as grateful guests, amicably chatting with everyone they met. They seemed to relish the contrast of this occasion with what they probably knew back home in an urban environment. Hilda, meanwhile, moved about getting photographs of the visitors mixing with Lucy's family. The actor's three-year old son, Free, played with other children who also were present. Except for a brief demonstration of his skill in the martial arts, Carradine kept a low profile and responded to the occasional question directed his way. He did so, that is, until deciding to take a swim in the swollen creek nearby.

Perhaps assuming his hosts customarily disrobed for such purposes with little attention to anyone present, Carradine casually stripped and strode into the water for a swim. At Lucy's request, the older children hurriedly rounded up the young ones and, eyes averted, provided the actor with the privacy ordinarily expected for swimming of this nature.

The romantic literature often leads readers to believe that this was the way "natural" people go about swimming, so I could appreciate how people of goodwill might unwittingly violate custom. But all this transpired quickly, and everyone's attention was diverted to something new that unfolded.

One of the visitors suggested that Lucy be pictured presenting a pipe to the actor. Directed to an open space, Lucy was positioned upright as Carradine (now clothed) fell to his knees, arms outstretched, in front of her. Repeatedly corrected by younger family members as to how one should hold the pipe for such a pose, Lucy was finally photographed. A kind of dramatic passing on of her father's spiritual legacy was thus staged, the photos of which perhaps were used later on for advertising purposes in cities far away. Immediately following Lucy's debut as pipe-holder, the guests bade farewell and drove to Rapid City in order to connect with their respective flights home.

The fruits of this encounter between Hollywood and Lucy's family ripened shortly after, and the play *Black Elk Speaks* was performed in a number of cities. *Tulsa World* columnist Danna Sue Walker reported the following on November 18, 1983:

Carradine visited the Black Elk wilderness in South Dakota with Chris Sergel, who authored the play, and with Neihardt's daughter, Hilda. . . . Carradine said the group met with Black Elk's granddaughter, Lisa Long Hill, and Lucy Looks Twice. Lisa performed the peace pipe ceremony with the three, and Carradine was made to promise he would play the part of Black Elk. The two women thought Carradine sounded much like Black Elk. [Actually, Lisa's name was Lone Hill, and she was Black Elk's great-granddaughter.]

A brochure put out by the American Indian Theatre Company also reported that "Carradine discussed *Black Elk Speaks* with Lucy Looks Twice, daughter of the holy man. She gladly gave Carradine permission to play her father in the play." Both the columnist and the brochure mentioned that plans were underway to film the production.

As early as the fall of 1976, the play had been performed, with Lisa having a small part. Lucy herself had even been flown to Washington, D.C., as an honored guest of the production. When I inquired as to how she felt about the course of events, Lucy expressed ambivalence. Extended family members were excited about involvement with the play, and Lucy too was provided with travel opportunities and attention that previously had not been part of her life. Accepting the script as simply a work based on her father's early life, she saw its importance in terms of calling attention to her people's history. She said that there was interest in the play, "since [my father] was a witness to the Wounded Knee massacre." In her opinion, the twentieth-century part of her father's life was on another level entirely and was pretty much disconnected from concerns addressed by the play. In this sense, she walked a path already pioneered by her father.

Resurrection of the nineteenth-century image of Black Elk relies heavily on its romantic appeal, and bolstering this appeal is a portrayal of the holy man as a resolute traditionalist who repudiates the alienating, technological world so foreign to his youth. Ethnic resurgence, literature, and drama provide staying power for such a characterization, and as shown, the human appetite for this type of representation seems to persist. The effort in this book, however, has been to reach a deeper understanding of how persons like Black Elk came to terms with conflict generated by the clashing of cultures.

Most of Black Elk's life was occupied with issues of the twentieth-century reservation era, and his energies were directed at concerns that still prevail today. His grieving

later in life was not nativistic retreatism, for he had confronted as much as anybody and still retained "the power
to live" meaningfully in a world far different from the one
of his youth. The sadness he experienced was because
"some [were] not even trying to catch it."

Words attributed to the holy man have been invoked to
rally his people from social torpor, and application of his
thought in this regard is legitimate. Black Elk was not re-
luctant to verbalize strongly felt sentiments, and his strategy for renewal was framed within the religious perspective. That is, challenging his people was well within his
sense of mission. His prescription for adjustment was religious, with social or political agendas flowing from what
he deemed foremost—a spiritual base.

Neither Brown nor Neihardt addressed the social milieu
of the aging holy man. Instead, readers were presented the
timeless portrait of an elder, suspended in nostalgia and
melancholy, hermetically insulated from his people's twentieth-century plight. Readers were left to imagine what this
social disenfranchisement entailed, as specific issues were
nowhere reported. Thematic to both works is an image of
nineteenth-century Sioux imprisoned within their reservation borders, waiting for, as Neihardt said, yesterday. Much
more, however, needed to be stated if Black Elk's life was
to be fully understood.

According to Fools Crow, the 1930s were: "the worst ten
years I know of . . . because of problems caused by intoxi-
cated people. . . . [S]uch shameful behavior. . . . [At a
gathering of holy-men] we discussed many things, but in
the end concluded that the solution was not in our hands,
that all we could do for the moment was to fall back on our
prayers" (Mails and Chief Eagle 1979:148–49). This meeting of native holy men, which included Black Elk, is central to understanding what undergirded their worldview.
Strategies for social change came after, or flowed from, a
religious foundation.

A Sioux social worker commented upon the high alcoholism rate at Pine Ridge (80–95 percent), and her discouragement is a kind of updated Black Elk, who, during his own life, witnessed the problem arise.[20] The social worker's observation is cited merely for the purpose of conveying a sense of the holy man in practical terms—minus the generalized symbols and images of his persona in *Black Elk Speaks* and *The Sacred Pipe*. The issue addressed here is one that he knew well, and the holy men tried to avert its spread by resolutely steering their energy in the direction they considered to be of foremost importance. The social worker commented that:

People still sit around crying about how it's all the white man's fault for bringing us firewater. Well, five generations later, we better start taking some responsibility ourselves— because we are committing self-genocide, breeding a new generation of idiots. If it keeps up at this rate, 50 years from now there won't be a Sioux on the reservation who can think straight even if he is sober. (Talbert 1986:9B).[21]

Nothing as pointed as the above appears in Black Elk quotations, and as a result, room has been left for interpreting him in broad, humanistic or nativistic terms. Such were, however, the kinds of concerns that confronted and discouraged him in later life, to which he applied his religious solution. Essentially, Black Elk was a social critic who derived his own strength and inspiration from the Lakota-Catholic religious sphere and who, in turn, used that framework to challenge his people unto renewal. As early as 1907, he was aware that his task of fostering and maintaining this religious consciousness would not be easy. A March 15 letter of his reads in part: "I spoke mainly on Jesus—when he was on earth, the teachings and his sufferings. I, myself, do a lot of these things. I suffer, and I try to teach my people the things that I wanted them to learn, but it's never done. . . . [Y]ou know when one sheep is surrounded with wolves, it has no place to go. That's how we are. We are ready to be eaten up" *(Sinasapa Wocekiye Taeyanpaha).* Black Elk's life and thought were indeed consistent with the leitmotif of Lakota culture and the basic spiritual posture its holy men tried to preserve.

Religious practice played an important, perhaps underestimated role within the strategies of adaptation to life on the Plains.[22] It had served the people well. With multifaceted changes accosting Pine Ridge, Black Elk had little else to offer as a life-giving alternative.

With the gradual loss of this reflexive religious disposition, Lakota culture was truly undergoing a major modification. As Mekeel's study noted after the Neihardt visit, "oriented by the particular times of their childhood and early youth, people born in different eras of Pine Ridge history [held] widely differing attitudes" (1935:5). Primary among these differences were religious practice and the Lakota religious perspective toward life itself. Religion had been something far more than just an aspect of culture for this people. It was instrumental in nurturing their ability to confront change. Black Elk's life clearly demonstrates this, as he represented a senior generation for whom "the Sacred [was] not an epiphenomenon, or secondary expression of reality; it [was] the deepest aspect of reality" (Grim 1983:4).

Given this new understanding of Black Elk, further inquiry can be carried forth in many directions. How, for example, did denominations within Christianity effectively communicate their doctrines to the Lakota (and other groups)?[23] To what extent were Native practitioners at odds with, or compliant to, the teachings administered by different denominations? In what specific ways did governmental agencies impede or promote the varying denominational agendas? What was the recidivism rate of medicine men who became church leaders, and why did this occur? What social factors challenged, as never before, the long-standing Lakota reliance on the sacred (however defined)? And how is this reliance, or basic approach to life, evident today, despite pressures that militate against it? Such are the types of questions embedded within the completed portrait of Black Elk. Nonetheless, as important and intriguing as such considerations might be, the over-riding concern here has been to set forth an examination of Black Elk's life that is empirically verifiable.

Readers of the earlier Black Elk material were left to ponder the complexity of the holy man. In the end, however, his life and thought are fairly straightforward. Those who have chosen instead to hunt for something more sublime will, as before, never catch it.

Lucy (Black Elk) Looks Twice modeling Lakota
powwow shawl, moccasins, beaded earrings, and
medallion, 1975.

▼

▼

Epilogue

Lucy Looks Twice, the last surviving child of Black Elk, died on April 23, 1978. She was consoled to know that the content of her father's thought had been captured in these pages.

Lucy was ill for a long time before she died, and on several occasions I confided that her passing would leave a void in my life. I encouraged her to hold out against the ravages of infirmity. So much had been exchanged during our visits. Many persons, places, and thoughts were raised in conversation by me, an inquisitive grandchild from a far different background, with her, a reassuring grandmother who tempered my emotion and concerns with a wisdom that conveyed solace.

To a great extent, the accounts here have filled that anticipated void, for they are a legacy telling of the infinite woven within the finite concerns of everyday Lakota, and indeed all, human life. As such, Lucy, her father, and his friends still speak. They do so to readers still en route to the land of many lodges.

▼

▼

Notes

Preface

1. "Lakota," the preferred term today, is linguistically more precise than the word "Sioux," but the latter is still used. See chapter 1 for a full discussion of this nomenclature.

2. Although its pagination differs from that of the two earlier editions, the Pocket Book reprint of *Black Elk Speaks* (1972) is cited in this text because for some time it has been commonly available to readers. References to this edition are abbreviated as *BES*.

3. Although translations of Wakan Tanka vary, "Great Spirit" is the one most commonly heard (today interchangeable with "God"), a supernatural creator-figure perceived as the source of all power.

4. The charge has been made that Neihardt, a nationally acclaimed poet, embellished Black Elk's observations—as Sally McClusky (1972), among others, has indicated. DeMallie's publication of Neihardt's field notes (1984b) helped clarify this issue, but *Black Elk Speaks* still remains a classic description of the Oglala worldview.

5. Powers appropriately titled an article "When Black Elk Speaks, Everybody Listens" (1990), as the following citations suggest. Norman Perrin, a biblical scholar at the University of Chicago, drew upon Black Elk for purposes of cross-cultural comparison vis-à-vis New Testament writers (1974). Willoya and Brown invoked the holy-man to support their doc-

177

trine of a universal religion (1962). Steinmetz (1980), after Duratschek (1974), argued that the holy-man exemplifies a phase in the evolution of theological reflection. Vine Deloria, Jr. argued that "God is Red" (1969), Black Elk articulating a pan-Indian spirituality quite distinct from notions associated with "white" religion. Sculptor Marshall M. Fredericks honored Black Elk with a bronze monument, and F. W. Thomsen depicted the holy man's vision on a memorial tower overlooking Dana College in Blair, Nebraska. Poet Donna Duesel de la Torriente produced *Bay Is The Land (To Black Elk)* (1982), a work claiming to be "an astounding proclamation made by a white American about the long-awaited dream of Black Elk." Leanin' Tree and Sunrise Publications (who accent their work with a "back-to-nature" motif) likewise peppered their products with quotations from the holy man. Where psychologist Carl Jung theorized about and directly referred to Black Elk (1970:206), novelist Thomas Berger was more covert. Readers of his *Little Big Man* (1964) (and viewers of the subsequent motion picture) were entranced by the story's pivotal character, Old Lodge Skins—a pseudonym, it seems, for Black Elk à la Neihardt. Such gnosticism was not required in 1979 when actor David Carradine was cast in the lead role of a largely fictionalized Black Elk. David Humphreys Miller produced two books (1957, 1959) that describe the Ghost Dance and Custer's fate from the viewpoint of Indian witnesses, the holy man being one of his key consultants. Hassrick's standard ethnography of the Sioux (1964) notes Brown and Neihardt as basic resources, while a contemporary analysis of Oglala religion (Powers 1974) cites the Black Elk material as authoritative. Moon's 1982 best-seller *Blue Highways,* a first-person account of traveling across modern America, noted *Black Elk Speaks* as a kind of intimate, literary traveling companion. Kehoe's study of the Ghost Dance (1989) devoted an entire chapter to the holy man's key role within contemporary revitalization efforts. Although not related to the patriarch, Wallace Black Elk no doubt caught the reading public's eye in 1990 with his handsome volume, ambiguously entitled *Black Elk,* which contained the religious perspective of this modern-day "shaman." Anthropologist William Lyon suggested (incorrectly, as later will be shown) that readers could regard Wallace as representing his namesake's spiritual legacy. Other books and articles (e.g., Capps 1976; Tedlock & Tedlock 1975), too numerous to list here, simply echo what this summary suggests. Finally, *Black Elk Speaks* has been published in German, Flemish, Dutch, Italian, Danish, Serbo-Croatian, Swedish, and Spanish.

6. For years, Ben was known as the "other face" on Mount Rushmore because of his popularity there with tourists. Ben had also appeared in motion pictures. This Black Elk, the media favorite, was the man some associated with books. *Healing of Memories* by Dennis and Matthew

Lynn (1974) quotes *The Sacred Pipe* and in a footnote does, in fact, erroneously attribute authorship to Ben.

7. Gretchen Bataille's article "Black Elk–New World Prophet" quotes Neihardt saying the holy man was "kind of a preacher"—an ambiguous rendering of what Neihardt meant and of Black Elk's style (1984:139). He was not "preachy," as such a reference might imply.

8. The title of *Black Elk's Story* (Rice 1991) probably captivates readers like the aforementioned (and equally misleading) *Black Elk* (Lyon and Black Elk 1990), this "armchair ethnology" being an example of just such speculation.

9. Holy Rosary Mission, founded by the Jesuits in 1888, continues today as a major educational institution of the Pine Ridge Reservation. Calling an older person grandmother or grandfather is a respectful gesture in Lakota tradition. This practice will surface again in a consideration of Lakota prayer that begins "Tunkashila Wakan Tanka," or "Grandfather Great Spirit." Similarly, in treaty gatherings, the president of the United States was referred to as grandfather. Chapter 1 discusses the importance of kin term usage among the Lakota.

10. Over the course of time, smaller grandchildren repeatedly—and delightfully—interrupted my visits, despite the seclusion of the pine bough shade.

11. Wallace Black Elk (cited earlier in reference to his book) was active with the American Indian Movement's occupation of Wounded Knee in 1973, and I assumed he was related in some way to Lucy's father. I inquired about his identity and was emphatically told that Wallace was no relation. The Black Elk name was regularly in the news during this very difficult time, and so Lucy was all the more anxious to have her father's life reported in its entirety (and not have his name confused with anyone else's). Curiously, William Lyon refers to the senior holy-man as Nick and to his contemporary coauthor as Black Elk—a form of address not employed by Lakota of the modern era (even though stereotypes would suggest otherwise).

12. Lucy's bias, if it could be called that, was simply to tell what she knew about her father's life. Whatever she reported (apart from family matters) was corroborated by Black Elk's former acquaintances.

chapter one
▼
Lakota Culture

1. The Algonquian word may have carried the more generic meaning "enemy" (Gallatin 1836). Others, meanwhile, have proposed that the word was derived from the French *sou* (or *sous*), a coin of minimal worth (again, a caricature of the people).

2. While practicing my Lakota vocabulary, I was corrected by a young person who said I was mispronouncing certain words—whereupon I was introduced to the Dakota dialect with my *l*'s replaced by the person's *d*'s. I was reminded of Lucy's experience as a child when she returned from Marty, South Dakota, and was teased for speaking with a slightly different accent. (See chapter 5, in which Lucy says: "I talked like a Yankton.")

3. Prairie/woodland people also refer to "council fires," so the metaphor may date back to when the ancestors of the Lakota lived in the eastern forests. The Assiniboine formerly were associated with the Nakota but split from this group during the early historical period. Henceforward they were referred to as rebels.

4. Although Plains cultures are frequently referred to as buffalo cultures, many non-Indian (and even Indian) peoples would be hard-pressed to elaborate the specifics listed here. Clearly, more than a source of food was lost with the disappearance of this animal (Dary 1974; *Wind River Rendezvous* 1983).

5. Later religious practice often aligned itself with the different camp memberships.

6. Lucy did not know these people, who were friends of her brother, Ben.

7. Place-names in Ontario, Canada, include the word "Sioux" (e.g., Sioux Lookout, Sioux Narrows) and are associated with this more eastern origin. Apart from the "emergence myth" origin story, one (perhaps of less antiquity) tells of a long journey from the banks of an eastern body of salt water (presumably the Atlantic Ocean) to a region with large bodies of fresh water (the Great Lakes) where bark lodges were erected (the early historical, woodland period).

8. Lucy's courtship and marriage in the 1920s still generally reflected the traditions reported here (see chapter 7).

9. In light of this cultural vocabulary, Catholic references to Fathers, Sisters, Brothers, and God's children resonated well with Lakota listeners (see chapter 4). This cornerstone of the Lakota worldview is detailed here because of implications related to "belonging" within the new world of twentieth-century reservation life. "Making relatives" (i.e., creating "fictive" kin) was too important to be restricted by skin color, and so this "familializing" of others accompanied the people into the contact period (and beyond).

10. Throughout the chapters that follow, individuals are periodically referred to by kin terms on the basis of the system described here and not necessarily, as one might assume, on bloodline (i.e., consanguinity).

11. In the midst of a face-off between Crazy Horse's people and the army, one of the former confronted the latter by riding up, warbonnet in place, and stopping the column. In what would appear to be a very tense moment, the rider said: "Let's dismount and have a smoke. Even a man about to die takes time to smoke" (i.e., partakes in a religious observance). Cf. Clark 1976:63.

chapter two
▼
Genealogy

1. Lucy's account might be regarded as an early twentieth-century experience of traditional Lakota "camp life" described in chapter 1.

2. This same information is given in *Black Elk Speaks* (53); page 199, however, mentions only one brother and one sister. "Give me eighty men and I would ride through the whole Sioux nation" was the boast of Captain William J. Fetterman before his command's annihilation on December 21, 1866, near Fort Phil Kearny in Montana. This so-called Fetterman Massacre is what Lucy refers to as the "battle of the one hundred slain"—the old Lakota way of describing this incident of Red Cloud's War (1866–68). The now-controversial Fort Laramie Treaty ended this conflict, as the United States was forced to accede to Lakota demands and withdraw from the Powder River country (Hebard and Brininstool 1922; Howard 1968; Hyde 1937; Olson 1965; Vestal 1932). For the past hundred years, a claim to the Black Hills was pressed by different Lakota groups, and a judgment was finally rendered on their behalf. Instead of the monetary settlement offered, some of the people insist upon a return of the land itself, which has prompted further litigation.

3. E.g., Black Elk's father (DeMallie 1984b:102), Lucy's half-brothers (13), and Black Elk's second wife (23). William and John were given the birth names of Never Showed Off and Good Voice Star, respectively; cf. Pine Ridge census rolls, 1893, 1896, and 1901 (National Archives and Records Service, Record Group 75, Microcopy M595, rolls 365, 367, and 368). The baptismal records of Holy Rosary Mission also contain such information along with occasional comments inscribed by the priests.

4. Mainline Christian denominations today, especially Roman Catholicism after Vatican II, express orthodoxy in ways different than in Black Elk's time. Curiously, the institutional model of Black Elk's Catholicism, which was more formalist than personalistic in its ritual and teachings, seems to have had a persuasive appeal that many adherents of later years did not appreciate as readily as Black Elk did.

5. The addition Lucy might be referring to is discussed in chapter 6.

6. Neihardt's terminology is at variance with this usage in the sense that Black Elk's designation as *pejuta wicasa* was more apt for the period covered in *Black Elk Speaks*. That is, the subtitle should have referred to Black Elk as a medicine man, not a holy man.

7. *The Sixth Grandfather* reports Black Elk saying that Kills the Enemy

was named One Side because of "his hair being cut on one side," and that ever since appearing this way in Black Elk's vision, he has been "One Side" (235). DeMallie mentions that Neihardt minimized "the imagery of warfare and killing" in the finished text (1984b:53), which could be another reason for avoiding the name "Kills the Enemy." Warrior hairstyles of the historic period could be the inspiration of such a name, but a more likely explanation might be found in Riggs's mention of an "antinatural" force or entity behind the *heyoka* practice. According to Riggs, "He is represented as a little old man with a cocked hat on his head"—a description exactly matching how Kills Enemy comported himself (quoted in Buechel 1970:174), a behavior quite consistent with Kills Enemy's long-standing *heyoka* identity.

8. Black Elk may have chosen his daughter's name as a devotion to Saint Lucy, whose name means "light." Within Catholic tradition, her assistance is sought by those having eye trouble.

9. In a 1991 interview, medicine man Pete Catches said, "There are a lot of fake medicine men . . . they have no power, no sacred reason, no spiritual contact" (Jeltz 1991). See chapter 4 for a discussion of Pete's religious practice.

10. See also Del Barton's novel *A Good Day to Die* (1980). The 1990 motion picture *Flatliners*, a film dealing with life-after-death experiences, begins with one of its characters saying, "Today is a good day to die," which further illustrates the continued currency of Black Elk material.

chapter three
▼
Conversion

1. Visiting Black Elk's coworker stirred sadness within me, and I felt a great deal of sympathy for the old man. As with Lucy, for example, a kind of kinship developed when, over time, she addressed me as *takoja* (grandchild). Similarly, with John, calling him "grandfather" seemed very natural soon after our visit began.

2. Jesuit history attributes the Lakota invitation to Pine Ridge and Rosebud as part of a tradition related to DeSmet's revered stature among the people. Critics of this interpretation argue that the Lakota request had nothing to do with religion but was actually a political ploy. That is, since the government had given jurisdiction of Pine Ridge to the Episcopalian church, the insistence upon Jesuit presence was simply a form of Lakota resistance in the guise of religion. Lucy mentioned that her father respected Red Cloud because of his decision to request Jesuits, and for his "choosing the 'Blackrobes' to teach the children of his people."

3. These archives will hereafter be noted as MACIM. They contain the

diaries cited, the Sialm citations, the *Indian Sentinel,* and the missionary newspaper *Sinasapa Wocekiye Taeyanpaha.*

4. According to Holy Rosary Mission's baptismal records, the famous Chief Red Cloud was christened "Peter," since he was, as Christianity says of the apostle Peter, first in rank among his people.

5. C. M. Weisenhorn wrote an obituary for Lindebner (on file at the Marquette Archives) that reported the following: "Towards the very end, he seemed to have forgotten every language but that of his apostolic labors and he spoke and prayed only in Lakota Sioux. 'Maria omakigago! Wakantanka imacuwo!' "Mary help! Lord take me!"

6. Forty-one band-derived communities were located on the Pine Ridge Reservation in 1935.

7. Given Lindebner's fluency in Lakota, it is questionable whether he addressed Black Elk in English on this occasion.

8. DeMallie (1984b:10) mentioned that Black Elk was baptized Episcopalian (at least nominally) as early as 1886, a requirement for participation in Buffalo Bill Cody's traveling show.

9. William Lyon, coauthor of *Black Elk,* states he has reason to believe otherwise (1990:xiii), though gives no evidence. Exegesis of the earlier Black Elk material has been open-ended and thus has permitted assertions such as these.

10. Raised within the Catholic tradition, I was not inspired when I heard the story and was perplexed by information that seemed contradictory. That is, I knew of the high regard bestowed by older Lakota upon many of the first-generation Jesuits, and yet this type of confrontational interaction did not seem very endearing.

11. Sialm's diary (no. 54) reported an experience Black Elk had with Lindebner that captured both the priest's style and one of the reasons why the catechist held him in such high regard. Black Elk said: "We were three men at the little church at Potato Creek. Father Lindebner cooked for us three with his little stove. He could cook for only one man at a time. First he cooked and gave it to me. Then he cooked for the second man. And lastly he cooked for himself."

12. Father Zimmerman's obituary for Black Elk in the October 1950 issue of the *Indian Sentinel* recounted his understanding of the holy-man's conversion in the following fashion: "Finally, the ice was broken. [He] became curious about the new religion, then interested, and at length professed his willingness to . . . be baptized" (102). A similarly unextraordinary course of events was reported by John Lone Goose, who said that Sam Kills Brave's entreaty simply led Black Elk to receive instruction from Father Aloysius Bosch, S.J., and that his lessons occurred at Manderson during the priest's frequent visits.

Certain persons, events, and interpretations within *The Sixth Grand-*

father do not match the accounts provided here. Where DeMallie reports that Black Elk's medicine practice "quickly brought him into conflict with the missionaries," Lucy said her father did not meet any Jesuits until his conversion. DeMallie also relates that Black Elk told Neihardt "that once, when he was performing a ceremony, a Jesuit priest arrived and destroyed the sacred objects he used in his curing. The patient recovered, but the priest was killed soon after by falling from a horse" (1984b:12). Ironically, the only priest on record to have died at Holy Rosary after falling from a horse was Father Bosch, the priest to whom John Lone Goose attributed much of Black Elk's instruction. Furthermore, Father Bosch died five months after the injury was sustained (although dying five months after the alleged incident perhaps may be considered "soon" when dealing with retributive religious justice). Disparate recollections of people and events possibly became misconstrued or reinterpreted either by Lucy or John or were somewhere mangled within the flow from the holy man, through his interpreter-son Ben, to Neihardt's notes many decades after the fact.

13. *IS* is the abbreviation for the *Indian Sentinel*, the "Official Organ of the Catholic Indian Missions," published out of Washington, D.C., and now no longer produced.

chapter four
▼
Catechist

1. DeMallie states that Black Elk missed the annual congress in 1931 because it coincided with the last two days of Neihardt's visit; the senior catechist's absence from the event was "no doubt conspicuous" (1984b:46). With the rest of his family at the congress, Black Elk probably attended the final day, once Ben bid farewell to the Neihardts (48). Whether he did or not, one's absence on such occasions was, in fact, not out of the ordinary.

2. Chapter 1 noted the importance among the Lakota of establishing kin. The Catholic terminology here represents a convergence of cultural systems that aided rapport. Lucy mentioned that her father called Lindebner not only "short Father" but also "little brother," an affective term for the man with whom he worked so closely.

3. I did hear about Black Fox later on from one elderly Manderson resident who claimed Black Fox was gifted in (among other things) telling the exact age of any stranger.

4. References to "prayer" by Lakota speakers can be ambiguous, since the same word refers both to an individual's prayers and to one's denominational affiliation.

5. A distant, aged relative of Black Elk's recalled that at one time "Nick

had fifty head of cattle." In fact, before the First World War, Lakota cattle-raising was quite successful, making the allotment of rations almost unnecessary.

6. The early Jesuits of both missions were predominantly German born, as reflected in this regular menu item. Black Elk's receptivity of the German Jesuits may very well have been aided by his familiarity with Germany itself, a country he visited while in Buffalo Bill's Wild West Show.

7. Bible passages and hymns were translated into Lakota by early missionaries, and Lucy's reference is to such a collection. Stephen R. Riggs of the Congregational church was a missionary of forty-two years among the Lakota who compiled a text of the Bible, hymns, and other literature in the Lakota dialect before his death in 1882. Further linguistic work was done by Franz Boas and Ella Deloria. Before these labors, Lakota had been an unwritten language.

8. The papal letter of May 15, 1956, "Haurietis Aquas," encouraged Catholics to maintain the traditional devotion to the "Sacred Heart of Jesus," and Lucy had been trained from early childhood to recite certain prayers associated with what this was intended to symbolize, namely, Christian love. Theresa Martin (1873-97), known to Catholics as "the Little Flower of Jesus," was a Carmelite nun recognized by the church as a saint in 1925. Devotion to her was particularly strong in Catholic circles during the time Nick Jr. was ill.

9. Waking up his wife in the middle of the night by pretending to look blindly in another direction might have been Black Elk's way of encouraging her to leave a light on.

chapter five
▼
Missionary

1. Lucy's reference is to the Native American Church; cf. La Barre 1969.

2. Black Elk's children Agatha and Mary died at the same time.

3. DeMallie (1984b:38) notes that Father Buechel denounced the Rabbit Dance at the 1929 Congress (the priest reportedly said it was one of the "chief evils threatening the family"). Not to be construed as caricature, Buechel's comments were part of a larger address entitled "What Must Be Done to Preserve the Indian Race?" The breakup of family life was the theme of his presentation, and among the chief evils contributing to this were the dance, "hasty marriages and the spirit of idleness among the young people" (*IS* 1929:151-52). Father Buechel left "the solution of the problem . . . entirely to the Indians." DeMallie noted that the Oglalas seemed to have agreed with Buechel, as they pledged to abstain from the

dance (Black Elk was one of the delegates). Interestingly, DeMallie's report on the Neihardt visit cites the occurrence of a Rabbit Dance! The catechist was a kind of cohost for the poet's entourage, but his precise role in orchestrating the visit is not clear. Neihardt's correspondence with government officials suggests, however, that this particular celebration was not Black Elk's idea (DeMallie 1984b:38–39).

4. The customary procedure at funerals is to wake the deceased at a meeting hall or a church for at least a night, with mourners present throughout the time until after burial, whereupon a "feed" is held for all present.

5. This type of exchange was perhaps cited in the pamphlet because of its apologetic content, as it shows Black Elk refuting the Protestant fundamentalist critique of Marian devotions among Catholics. This type of doctrinal conflict accompanied denominational presence among Indian peoples, who in turn were schooled to defend their new affiliation.

6. Father Perrig's diary entry of December 15, 1908, also notes that "James Grass and Nick Black Elk, who had gone to convert the Winnebagoes, returned after having achieved nothing."

7. In the Neihardt transcripts, Black Elk claims to have started the wearing of ghost shirts, but this practice is not confirmed in other documents of the period (DeMallie 1984b:262).

8. St. Peter's Church is thirteen miles north of present-day Manderson.

chapter six
▼
Life Story

1. The priest's diary reports the following curious exchange: "Black Elk asked F. Sialm: 'Do you understand the Indians?' Father answered with the question 'Do you, being an Indian yourself, do you understand them?' He said: 'No.'"

2. Forty years after Sialm stated this objection, McCluskey reported Neihardt as saying that the final three paragraphs of the book were what Black Elk "would have said if he had been able" (1979:232). Holler disagrees with Neihardt's opinion that these most-quoted passages of the work reflected the holy-man's thought (1984:36–37).

3. This letter may be the addition Lucy said her father gave Neihardt (see chapter 2).

4. Personal communication from both Brown and Catches.

5. An oblique reference to his children's discord is made when recounting his involvement in the Ghost Dance and in Wounded Knee: "At this time I had no children and maybe if I had been killed then I would have been better off" (DeMallie 1984b:275). Without the background provided here, readers would not understand why Black Elk offered this reflection.

6. See "Re: Nick Black Elk as 'veteran catechist'; 'Feast of Christ the King,' 1937, (appeal letters written by Joseph A. Zimmerman, S.J.)." In this same material, Zimmerman reports Black Elk's writing letters in 1934 that were related to the Neihardt material: "after the book was published he made in English and in Sioux formal statements of his Catholic faith signing them before witnesses" (MACIM).

7. Bones figure prominently in Lakota mythology, particularly within the story that relates the coming of the Sacred Pipe, wherein a character is reduced to skeletal remains for pursuing a self-centered course of action (Brown 1953:3–4). Melody suggests the meaning here is that "the life of [egocentric] gratification is itself that of bones" (1980:12). It is not surprising that Black Elk drew upon this conventional metaphor to illustrate a morality that was thematic in his life both before and after his conversion.

chapter seven
▼
Sacred Visions

1. Joining the litany of works related to the vision are *Keepers of the Fire: Journey to the Tree of Life, Based on Black Elk's Vision* (Eagle Walking Turtle 1989) and Time-Life Books, which featured the vision in a special series of works dealing with mysticism and the occult (1989).

2. Goll's black road ending in hell is green on some maps. John Lone Goose refers, like Goll, to a black road, whereas Lucy reported the map as having red and yellow roads. Different versions existed (the one pictured here, printed in India, was one of the standards employed at Pine Ridge).

3. These catechetical instruments are, in the literature, sometimes called ladders (Hanley 1965; Pipes 1936:237–40; Prucha 1988:130–37). Some were more crudely drawn than the ones used at Pine Ridge, and some were decidedly sectarian in their portrayal of Christian history.

4. Although colors carried conventional associations, latitude did exist for individual usage (i.e., colors could be multivocal). What they denoted often depended upon context—and the practitioner's inspiration. Additionally, it is not uncommon to hear Indian religious leaders today refer to the colors yellow, black, red, and white as representing the four "races" of humanity, which is often said to be a traditional association.

5. In an interview shortly before his death, Neihardt was asked if Black Elk's Catholicism "colored his thinking." His response: "It might have, here and there in spots, but fundamentally no" (taped interview of F. W. Thomsen with John Neihardt, Dana College, Blair, Nebraska).

6. This quotation may have been composed entirely by Neihardt, as it does not appear in the stenographic record. However, DeMallie mentions that some material is simply unable to be located (1984b:346n). Within the fieldwork setting, one often learns about matters in casual conversations, or through offhand remarks, and must rely on memory of the details discussed when sitting down to write. Because of the correspondence of the above quotation with Black Elk's experience, something of this nature may well have transpired.

7. For Black Elk's description of the Sun Dance, see Brown (1953:67–100). See also Leslie Spier (1921:451–527) for a cross-cultural analysis of this ritual. Until his death, Lucy's husband was one of the men responsible for finding and setting up a cottonwood tree for use in the yearly Sun Dance at Pine Ridge.

8. Before her death in 1936, Martha Bad Warrior, a ninety-nine-year-old keeper of the pipe and relative of Elk Head's, provided privileged information to Wilbur Riegert concerning the pipe. His account of this meeting was published posthumously in 1975 in Rapid City, South Dakota.

9. Green Grass, South Dakota, is a secluded community on the Cheyenne River Reservation, home of the Miniconju branch of western Lakota and the place where the original sacred pipe is kept (Steltenkamp 1982:38–49).

10. Iktomi is the spider, the trickster character of the Lakota.

11. Sung to the tune of the more traditional Christian hymn "Praise God from Whom All Blessings Flow," *Jesus Cante* (Heart of Jesus) is still popular among older Lakota Catholics.

12. Pine Ridge became a reservation in 1878 and was administered by the Episcopalian church, who established its mission in 1875 through the Grant administration's "Peace Policy." Lakota requests for "Blackrobes" were finally approved, and so the Jesuits arrived in 1888.

13. Regarding the loss of these children, Lucy said: "I felt bad for a long time, but Father Zimmerman was right there to comfort me. I always thought, 'God wants them. God took them.' He loved them so much that he didn't want them to go through what's coming in the future."

14. Leo died on November 21, 1974.

chapter eight
▼
Elder

1. Lucy also mentioned that her father "even owned a race horse at one time called 'Button.' He ran quarter mile. Later, he used him [as] a workhorse."

2. DeMallie says Black Elk started work for the pageant (begun in 1927) in 1935 or earlier (1984b:63).

3. John Gutzon de la Mothe Borglum (1867–1941) was the chief sculptor at Mount Rushmore.

4. Although Lucy said that the prayer he used for averting bad weather

was in his prayer book ("it means the same thing . . . that prayer is in the prayer book"), she may have meant the "sacramentary" text used at Catholic liturgies (which contains prayers for favorable weather). Weather control is reported elsewhere in North America as part of the shamanic vocation. See Landes 1971:134.

5. Leo was still alive at the time this interview took place, and Lucy's reference is to him. His mood was not pleasant that particular day.

6. This is a translation of the prayer Lucy uttered from memory in Lakota.

7. Norma Regina Looks Twice, granddaughter of Black Elk, died in the fall of 1978.

8. The store referred to here is just a short distance from the church—an indication of how slowly the two men must have walked (since the rosary prayers take some time to recite).

9. Powers stated in his study of *yuwipi* that "no one wearing a [Catholic] medal would be permitted to stay in the meeting. One man had a rosary in his pocket but was afraid to say so. Soon something in the darkness picked him up and threw him out the window" (1982:54). Ben Marrowbone said that *yuwipi* practitioners did not want "holy pictures" around because they were afraid of them. Different approaches to these types of ceremony seem to exist, given Little Warrior's use of such objects. The argument could be made that Little Warrior did not, strictly speaking, conduct a *yuwipi* practice. Steinmetz, however, classifies him as *yuwipi* (1990:26).

10. An annual tourist event held in the Black Hills town of Custer, South Dakota.

chapter nine
▼
Farewell

1. This celestial occurrence might have been the Perseid meteor shower, the most active and most visible of such phenomena in recent history.

2. Miller suggested that Black Elk's birth was even earlier than 1862 (1957:185), while his tombstone reads 1858.

3. Brother Siehr died in the spring of 1990 at Holy Rosary Mission.

4. John died November 23, 1975, and was buried at Manderson.

5. Cf. Brown 1953:10–30.

6. The Catholic church at Wounded Knee was one of the buildings occupied and considerably damaged, along with its contents. Occupation supporters regarded its ruin as legitimate symbolic protest, while Lucy regarded it as desecration, both of a religious place and of her father's memory.

chapter ten
▼
Evaluations

1. Ironically, when first published, neither *Black Elk Speaks* nor *The Sacred Pipe* attracted much attention.

2. Other Native groups also grapple with this issue, and Black Elk's image often has been enlisted to aid their effort. For example, Omaha spiritual leader Joe Kemp said that "Black Elk was a sacred man to whom *Indians* turned in time of need" (italics added). He offered this reflection to an audience at the ground-breaking ceremony for a Black Elk monument in Blair, Nebraska.

3. This sentimentality may be comparable to political rhetoric that invokes an idealized "spirit of democracy" existing among the nation's Founding Fathers.

4. One shortcoming with this approach is pointed out by Beatrice Medicine (1983:267–77). At Wounded Knee, a spokesman for the American Indian Movement said AIM was "a new warrior society," and this label was destined to capture imaginations. In rhetoric still fashionable among some Indian groups, he said that "white persons" conceive of warriors as the "armed forces . . . hired killers," but Indian people have "men and women of the nation who have dedicated themselves to give everything that they have to the people. A warrior should be the first one to go hungry or the last one to eat . . . the first one to give away his moccasins and the last one to get new ones. That type of feeling among Indian people is what a warrior society is all about. He is ready to defend his family in time of war—to hold off any enemy, and is perfectly willing to sacrifice himself to the good of his tribe and his people. That's what a warrior society is to Indian people." (*Akwesasne Notes* 1974:61–62).

5. The Mohawk occupation of Oka, Quebec, in 1990 revealed a willingness to continue to employ the militant strategy born at Wounded Knee. One of the keynote speakers at Lake Superior University's Conference on Indian Affairs (1991) proudly reported that fifteen-year-olds also manned the barricades at Oka and were willing to die for the principles championed by some of their elders. The speaker's position was not espoused by all Oka participants, who, as in the case of Wounded Knee, differed on which principles to champion.

Lucy drew upon the warrior metaphor, too, but in a way that conflicts with the earlier stereotype of her father. She said his contemporary message would be "to call the people to religion . . . 'teach your children prayers, see that they go to church; that's the only way—the church and the family . . . to be children of God and soldiers for Christ. You must stand the ground and make the fight.'"

6. Although *The Trial of Billy Jack* carried a disclaimer that its similarity to persons living or dead was purely coincidental, the film did in fact dramatize (with names and places changed) a major incident that led to the occupation of Wounded Knee, namely, the killing of Raymond Yellow Thunder at an American Legion Hall in Gordon, Nebraska. More recent films such as *War Party,* released in 1989, continue this type of characterization with a decidedly militant theme. The youthful protagonists of this modern-day story are encouraged by a religious elder to charge their horses at the trigger-ready National Guard (equivalently to commit suicide). The movie thus concludes with the youths reenacting a Blackfeet attack, in which they died. (Such an attack was perceived as the sole option for Blackfeet, and for like-minded "warriors" of today.) Interestingly, Dennis Banks, a leader of the Wounded Knee occupation, appeared as a character in the film.

7. Social protest in the style of Martin Luther King or Gandhi has not elicited the widespread response that these armed confrontations have garnered, perhaps because of the entrenched warrior stereotyping described here. The "new Indian wars" of recent years, however, have been "fought" by Native people in the courtroom and by those who have assumed decision-making roles in religious, educational, health, and human service fields.

8. Both Indian and African American groups have experienced a loss of ethnic identity, which the "pride in heritage" trend has sought to redress.

9. Deloria's work challenged Christian churches to "inculturate" their religious practices even further. As a result of his critique and that of others, some denominations have been more sensitive to not confusing theological dogma with ascetic and cultural observances from the older tradition.

10. This relative did not wish to be identified in this text for fear of reprisal arising from her comments. A "woman of few words," rugged, and forceful in tone, she digressed little and did not mince her words.

11. *The New Indians,* produced in 1987 by the National Geographic Society. Conference quotations are from this film.

12. DeMallie notes that discussions of this topic usually dissolve "into political rhetoric rather than objective assessment" (1984b:80).

13. The government's 1894 survey of Indians stated that medicine men wielded much influence at Pine Ridge especially.

14. Short Bull was a leading proponent of the Ghost Dance, along with Kicking Bear, his brother-in-law. According to Jesuit tradition, Sword would visit with Father Digmann and discuss theological matters at great length.

15. Sectarian affiliation was not unlike sodality memberships within the older tradition (see chapter 1). In fact, a certain competitiveness, exclu-

sivity, or special identity seems to have been associated with such participation in both the old and the new orders.

16. This same theme is apparent in a study among the modern Tswana of Southern Africa. See Alverson 1978.

17. Bucko indicated that Black Elk's extended reflections on the meanings and symbols of the sweatlodge ritual are the first of any length within the literature. Previous material had "focused on the many pragmatic uses of the sweat lodge." However, after this initial theologizing, subsequent writings have expanded the interpretive script articulated by practitioners and investigators (Bucko 1992:85). Lucy mentioned that Buechel's long-standing relationship with Black Elk included many hours of theological discussion, interaction that perhaps moved Black Elk to emphasize symbolic meanings that earlier accounts did not contain. Codification, or standardization, was more the tradition of his Catholic practice than that of his Lakota heritage (134). Steinmetz mentions that Fools Crow, a practicing Catholic, "formed many of his Lakota Christian beliefs on his own, without the assistance of a Catholic priest" (1990:8). This observation is consistent with information Lucy provided regarding her father's and her own experience.

18. Hultkrantz considers *The Sacred Pipe* "the most widely read work on Plains Indian religion" (Capps 1976:91). As such, it especially needs the caution offered here. An attempt to make Black Elk's thought in *The Sacred Pipe* something that it is not indicts researchers who "treat rites rather like a set of clues or a test to be solved by finding answers that all fit together. . . . as though the cry 'It fits' would convincingly repay the effort and ingenuity" (Lewis 1980:186).

19. MacGregor's reading of the early period would lead one to believe that all missionaries represented a ghoulish presence that attracted no one. (But then we would have to question why so many Lakota were devout participants within the different denominations.) In contrast, Duratschek's work tends to highlight the success of Catholic missionary efforts. One account offsets the other, but the social equation was more complicated than simply an interplay of missionaries and Indians. The reservation system included persons whose interests had nothing to do with, or were at cross-purposes to, the work undertaken by different denominations. The array of profiteers, bootleggers, transient government personnel, and other passersby lent a certain credibility to missionaries who remained over time. That is, their altruistic presence (or just their willingness to live in simplicity among the people), however appreciated, was not so ambiguous.

20. Black Elk himself did not consume alcohol.

21. Fetal alcohol syndrome is referred to here, as it has become a severe problem at Pine Ridge.

22. A similar argument is made for explaining the emergence of the Midé

Society among the Ojibway as a "tool" of adaptation during the historical period (Grim 1983:72–73).

23. Scholarly assessments of, polemics against, and apologias for Christian missionary efforts within Native North America are extensive. For a sampling, see Berkhofer 1965; Bowden 1981; Deloria 1973; Harrod 1971; and Moore 1982.

▼

▼

Bibliography

Akwesasne Notes (Mohawk Nation). 1974. *Voices from Wounded Knee: The People Are Standing Up*. Rooseveltown, N.Y.

Alverson, Hoyt. 1978. *Mind in the Heart of Darkness*. New Haven: Yale University Press.

Anderson, Gary Clayton. 1984. *Kinsmen of Another Kind: Dakota-White Relations in the Upper Mississippi Valley, 1650–1862*. Lincoln: University of Nebraska Press.

Baraga, R. R. 1973. *A Dictionary of the Otchipwe Language*. Minneapolis: Ross & Haines.

Barrett, Richard A. 1984. *Culture and Conduct: An Excursion in Anthropology*. Belmont, Calif.: Wadsworth Publishing.

Barton, Del. 1980. *A Good Day to Die*. New York: Doubleday.

Bataille, Gretchen M. 1984. "Black Elk—New World Prophet." In *A Sender of Words: Essays in Memory of John G. Neihardt*, ed. Vine Deloria, Jr. Salt Lake City: Howe Brothers.

Berger, Thomas. 1964. *Little Big Man*. New York: Dial Press.

Berkhofer, Robert F. 1965. *Salvation and the Savage: An Analysis of Protestant Missions and American Indian Response, 1787–1862*. Lexington: University of Kentucky Press.

————. 1978. *The White Man's Indian: Images of the American Indian from Columbus to the Present*. New York: Alfred A. Knopf.

Bogoras, Waldemar. 1965. "Shamanistic Performance in the Inner

195

Room." In *Reader in Comparative Religion: An Anthropological Approach*, ed. William A. Lessa and Evon Z. Vogt, 454–60. 2d ed. New York: Harper & Row.

Bourguignon, Erika. 1979. *Psychological Anthropology: An Introduction to Human Nature and Cultural Differences*. New York: Holt, Rinehart & Winston.

Bowden, Henry Warner. 1981. *American Indians and Christian Missions: Studies in Cultural Conflict*. Chicago: University of Chicago Press.

Brown, Dee. 1970. *Bury My Heart at Wounded Knee: An Indian History of the American West*. New York: Holt, Rinehart & Winston.

Brown, Joseph Epes. 1953. *The Sacred Pipe: Black Elk's Account of the Seven Rites of the Oglala Sioux*. Norman: University of Oklahoma Press. Reprint. Baltimore: Penguin Books, 1971.

————. 1979. "The Wisdom of the Contrary." *Parabola* 4 (no. 1): 54–65.

Brumble, H. David, III. 1981. *An Annotated Bibliography of American Indian and Eskimo Autobiographies*. Lincoln: University of Nebraska Press.

Bryde, John F. 1966. *The Sioux Indian Student: A Study of Scholastic Failure and Personality Conflict*. Vermillion: University of South Dakota.

Bucko, Raymond A. 1992. "Inipi: Historical Transformation and Contemporary Significance of the Sweat Lodge in Lakota Religious Practice." Ph.D. diss., University of Chicago, Department of Anthropology.

Buechel, Eugene. 1970. *A Dictionary of the Teton Dakota Sioux Language*. Edited by Paul Manhart. Pine Ridge, S.D.: Red Cloud Indian School.

————. 1978. *Lakota Tales and Texts*. Edited by Paul Manhart. Pine Ridge, S.D.: Red Cloud Indian School.

Capps, Walter Holden, ed. 1976. *Seeing with a Native Eye: Essays on Native American Religion*. New York: Harper Forum Books.

Castaneda, Carlos. 1968. *The Teachings of Don Juan: A Yaqui Way of Knowledge*. New York: Ballantine Books.

Catlin, George. 1844. *Letters and Notes on Manners, Customs, and Conditions of the North American Indian*. 4 vols. London: The Author. Reprint. New York: Dover Publications, 1973.

Chittenden, Hiram M., and Alfred T. Richardson. 1905. *Life, Letters, and Travels of Father Pierre Jean De Smet, S.J.* 4 vols. New York.

Clark, R. A. 1976. *The Killing of Chief Crazy Horse*. Lincoln: University of Nebraska Press.

Crapanzano, Vincent. 1977. "On the Writing of Ethnography." *Dialectical Anthropology* 2:69–73.

Dary, David A. 1974. *The Buffalo Book*. New York: Avon Books.

Deloria, Ella. 1944. *Speaking of Indians*. New York: Friendship Press.
————. N.d. "Teton Myths." American Philosophical Society MS. Franz Boas Collection.

Deloria, Vine, Jr. 1969. *Custer Died for Your Sins*. New York: Macmillan.
————. 1973. *God Is Red*. New York: Grosset & Dunlap.
————. 1979. "Introduction," *Black Elk Speaks*. Lincoln: University of Nebraska Press.

DeMallie, Raymond J. 1978. "Pine Ridge Economy: Cultural and Historical Perspectives." In *American Indian Economic Development*, ed. Sam Stanley, 237–312. The Hague: Mouton.
————. 1979. "Change in American Indian Kinship Systems, the Dakota." In *Currents in Anthropology: Essays in Honor of Sol Tax*, ed. Robert Hinshaw. The Hague: Mouton.
————. 1984a. "John G. Neihardt's Lakota Legacy." In *A Sender of Words: Essays in Memory of John G. Neihardt*, ed. Vine Deloria, Jr. Salt Lake City: Howe Brothers.
————. 1984b. *The Sixth Grandfather: Black Elk's Teachings Given to John G. Neihardt*. Lincoln: University of Nebraska Press.

Densmore, Frances. 1970. *Chippewa Customs*. Minneapolis: Ross & Haines.

DeVoto, Bernard, ed. 1953. *The Journals of Lewis and Clark*. Boston: Houghton Mifflin.

Dollard, John. 1935. *Criteria for the Life History*. New Haven: Yale University Press.

Dorsey, James Owen. 1894. *A Study of Siouan Cults*. Eleventh Annual Report of the Bureau of American Ethnology, pp. 351–544.
————. 1897. *Siouan Sociology*. Fifteenth Annual Report of the Bureau of American Ethnology, pp. 205–44.

Driver, Harold E. 1969. *Indians of North America*. Chicago: University of Chicago Press.

Duesel de la Torriente, Donna. 1982. *Bay Is the Land (to Black Elk)*. Reseda, Calif.: Mojave Books.

Dunsmore, Roger. 1977. "Nickolaus Black Elk: Holy Man in History." *Kuksu: Journal of Backcountry Writing*, no. 6:4–29.

Duratschek, Sister Mary Claudia. 1947. *Crusading along Sioux Trails: A History of the Catholic Indian Missions of South Dakota*. Yankton, S.D.: Grail.

Durkheim, Emile. 1965. *The Elementary Forms of the Religious Life*. New York: Free Press.

Eagle Walking Turtle. 1989. *Keepers of the Fire: Journey to the Tree of Life, Based on Black Elk's Vision*. Santa Fe: Bear & Company Publishing.

Eggan, Fred R. 1966. *The American Indian: Perspectives for the Study of Social Change*. Chicago: Aldine Press.

Erdoes, Richard, and John (Fire) Lame Deer. 1972. *Lame Deer: Seeker of Visions: The Life of a Sioux Medicine Man*. New York: Simon & Schuster.

Erikson, Erik. 1963. *Childhood and Society*. 2d ed. New York: W. W. Norton.

Faulkner, Virginia, and Frederick C. Luebke, eds. 1982. *Vision and Refuge: Essays on the Literature of the Great Plains*. Lincoln: University of Nebraska Press.

Feraca, Stephen E. 1961. "The Yuwipi Cult of the Oglala and Sicangu Teton Sioux." *Plains Anthropologist* 6:155-63.

————. 1962. "The Teton Sioux Eagle Medicine Cult." *American Indian Tradition* 8 (no. 5): 195-96.

Furlong, Jay. 1980. "The Occupation of Wounded Knee, 1973." Master's thesis, University of Oklahoma, Norman.

Gallatin, Albert S. 1836. *A Synopsis of the Indian Tribes within the United States East of the Rocky Mountains, and in the British and Russian Possessions in North America*. Transactions and Collections of the American Antiquarian Society, vol. 2.

Gearing, Fred. 1970. *The Face of the Fox*. Chicago: Aldine Publishing.

Geertz, Clifford. 1968. "Religion as a Cultural System." In *Anthropological Approaches to the Study of Religion*, ed. Michael Banton, 1-46. London: Tavistock.

————. 1973. *The Interpretation of Cultures*. New York: Basic Books.

Gessner, Robert. 1931. *Massacre*. New York: Cape & Smith.

Gill, Sam D. 1982. *Native American Religions: An Introduction*. Belmont, Calif.: Wadsworth Publishing.

Goddard, Ives. 1984. "The Study of Native North American Ethnonymy." In *Native American Naming Systems*, ed. Elizabeth Tooker. American Ethnological Society Proceedings 1980. New York.

Goll, Louis J. 1940. *Jesuit Missions among the Sioux*. St. Francis, S.D.: St. Francis Mission.

Grim, John A. 1983. *The Shaman*. Norman: University of Oklahoma Press.

Grobsmith, Elizabeth S. 1981. *Lakota of the Rosebud: A Contemporary Ethnography*. New York: Holt, Rinehart & Winston.

Hanley, Philip M. 1965. The Catholic Ladder and Missionary Activity in the Pacific Northwest. Master's thesis, University of Ottawa, faculty of Theology.

Harrod, Howard. 1971. *Mission among the Blackfeet*. Norman: University of Oklahoma Press.

Hassrick, Royal B. 1964. *The Sioux: Life and Customs of a Warrior Society*. Norman: University of Oklahoma Press.

Hebard, Grace Raymond, and E. A. Brininstool. 1922. *The Bozeman Trail: Historical Accounts of the Blazing of the Overland Route into the Northwest, and the Fights with Red Cloud's Warriors*. 2 vols. Cleveland: Arthur H. Clark.

Hill, Ruth Beebe. 1979. *Hanta Yo*. New York: Warren Books.

Holler, Clyde. 1984a. "Black Elk's Relationship to Christianity." *American Indian Quarterly*, Winter, 37–49.

————. 1984b. "Lakota Religion and Tragedy: The Theology of *Black Elk Speaks*." *Journal of the American Academy of Religion* 52 (no. 1): 19–45.

Hoover, Herbert T. 1979 *The Sioux: A Critical Bibliography*. Bloomington and London: Indiana University Press.

Howard, James H. 1968. *The Warrior Who Killed Custer: The Personal Narrative of Chief Joseph White Bull*. Lincoln: University of Nebraska Press.

Hunt, George T. 1967. *The Wars of the Iroquois: A Study in Intertribal Trade Relations*. Madison: University of Wisconsin Press.

Hyde, George E. 1937. *Red Cloud's Folk: A History of the Oglala Sioux Indians*. Norman: University of Oklahoma Press.

————. 1961. *Spotted Tail's Folk: A History of the Brulé Sioux*. Norman: University of Oklahoma Press.

Hyers, M. Conrad. 1969. *Holy Laughter: Essays on Religion in the Comic Perspective*. New York: Seabury Press.

James, William. 1961. *The Varieties of Religious Experience: A Study in Human Nature*. New York: Macmillian.

Jeltz, Patsy. 1991. "Elder Pete Catches Shares Wisdom." *Lakota Times*, July 24, B1.

Jung, C. G. 1970. *Mysterium Conjunctionis*. Princeton, N.J.: Princeton University Press.

Kardiner, Abram. 1945. *The Psychological Frontiers of Society*. New York: Columbia University Press.

Kehoe, Alice Beck. 1989. *The Ghost Dance, Ethnohistory and Revitalization*. New York: Holt, Rinehart & Winston.

Kemnitzer, Luis. 1969. "Yuwipi." *Pine Ridge Research Bulletin*, no. 10:26–33.

————. 1970. "Cultural Provenience of Objects Used in Yuwipi: A Modern Teton Dakota Healing Ritual." *Ethnos* 35:40–75.

Kenton, Edna. 1954. *The Jesuit Relations and Allied Documents*. New York: Vanguard Press.

Kluckhohn, Clyde. 1945. "The Personal Document in Anthropological Science." In *The Use of Personal Documents in History, Anthropology, and Sociology*, p. 29. Social Science Research Council, Bulletin 53. New York.

Kroeber, Karl. 1983. "Reasoning Together." In *Smoothing the Ground: Essays on Native American Oral Literature*, ed. Brian Swann, 347-64. Berkeley: University of California Press.

Krupat, Arnold. 1981. "The Indian Autobiography: Origins, Type, and Function." *American Literature* 53 (no. 1): 22-42.

La Barre, Weston. 1969. *The Peyote Cult*. New York: Schocken Books.

Lame Deer, John. 1972. *Lame Deer, Seeker of Visions*. New York: Simon & Schuster.

Landes, Ruth. 1971. *The Ojibwa Woman*. W. W. Norton.

Langness, L. L. 1965. *The Life History in Anthropological Science*. New York: Holt.

Langness, L. L., and Gelya Frank. 1981. *Lives: An Anthropological Approach to Biography*. Novato, Calif.: Chandler & Sharp, Publishers.

Lehmer, Donald J. 1977. "Selected Writings of Donald J. Lehmer." In *Reprints in Anthropology*, vol. 3. Lincoln, Nebr.

Lévi-Strauss, Claude. 1969. *The Elementary Structures of Kinship*. Boston: Beacon Press.

Lewis, Gilbert. 1980. *Day of Shining Red*. New York: Cambridge University Press.

Lewis, Thomas. 1970. "Notes on the Heyoka: The Teton Dakota 'Contrary' Cult." *Pine Ridge Research Bulletin*, no. 11:7-19.

Lincoln, Kenneth. 1983. "Native American Literatures," In *Smoothing the Ground: Essays on Native American Oral Literature*, ed. Brian Swann. Berkeley: University of California Press.

Linden, George W. 1983. "Black Elk Speaks as a Failure Narrative." Dakota History Conference.

Linden, George W., and Fred W. Robbins. 1982. "Mystic Medicine: Black Elk's First Cure." Dakota History Conference.

Linderman, Frank B. 1962. *Plenty-Coups: Chief of the Crows*. Lincoln: University of Nebraska Press.

Linton, Ralph. 1943. "Nativistic Movements." *American Anthropologist* 45:230-40.

Little Thunder, Jake. N.d. *Tiospaye*. Curriculum Materials Resource Unit, Oglala Sioux Culture Center, Red Cloud Indian School, Pine Ridge, S.D., in cooperation with Black Hills State College, Spearfish, S.D.

Lowie, Robert. 1948. *Social Organization*. New York: Rinehart.

———. 1963. *Indians of the Plains*. American Museum of Natural History. Garden City, N.Y.: Natural History Press.

Lynn, Dennis, and Matthew Lynn. 1974. *Healing of Memories*. Ramsey, N.J.: Paulist Press.

Lyon, William, and Wallace Black Elk. 1990. *Black Elk.* New York: Harper & Row.

McClusky, Sally. 1979. "Black Elk Speaks and So Does John Neihardt." *Western American Literature* 6:231–42.

MacGregor, Gordon. 1946. *Warriors without Weapons.* Chicago: University of Chicago Press.

McGregor, James H. 1940. *The Wounded Knee Massacre from the Viewpoint of the Sioux.* Baltimore: Wirth Brothers.

Mails, Thomas E., and Dallas Chief Eagle. 1979. *Fools Crow.* Garden City, N.Y.: Doubleday.

Marty, Martin. 1970. *Righteous Empire: The Protestant Experience in America.* New York: Dial Press.

Maynard, Eileen, and Gayla Twiss. 1969. *That These People May Live: Conditions among the Oglala Sioux of the Pine Ridge Reservation.* Community Mental Health Program, Pine Ridge Service Unit, Aberdeen Area, Indian Health Service, Pine Ridge, S.D.

Medicine, Bea[trice]. 1969. "The Changing Dakota Family." *Pine Ridge Research Bulletin,* no. 9 (June): 1–20.

———. 1983. "Warrior Women: Sex Role Alternatives for Plains Indian Women." In *The Hidden Half: Studies of Plains Indian Women,* ed. Patricia Albers and Beatrice Medicine, 267–77. Lanham, Md.: University Press of America.

Mekeel, Scudder. 1935. *The Economy of a Modern Teton Dakota Community.* New Haven: Yale University Press.

Melody, Michael E. 1980. "Lakota Myth and Government: The Cosmos as the State." *American Indian Culture and Research Journal* 4 (no.3 3): 1–19.

Miller, David Humphreys. 1957. *Custer's Fall.* New York: Bantam Book.

———. 1959. *Ghost Dance.* New York: Duell, Sloan, & Pearce.

Milligan, Edward A. 1973. *Wounded Knee 1973 and the Fort Laramie Treaty of 1868.* Bottineau, N.D.: Bottineau Courant Print.

Mirsky, Jeannette. 1966. "The Dakota." In *Cooperation and Competition among Primitive Peoples,* ed. Margaret Mead, 382–427, rev. ed. Boston: Beacon.

Momaday, N. Scott. 1984. "To Save a Great Vision." In *A Sender of Words: Essays in Memory of John G. Neihardt,* ed. Vine Deloria, Jr., 30–38, Salt Lake City: Howe Brothers.

Moon, William Least Heat. 1982. *Blue Highways: A Journey into America.* New York: Fawcett Crest.

Mooney, James. 1896. *The Ghost-Dance Religion and the Sioux Outbreak of 1890.* Smithsonian Institution, Bureau of American Ethnology, Annual Report, 14, pt. 2. Washington, D.C.

————. 1907. *The Cheyenne Indians.* Memoirs of the American Anthropological Association, vol. 1, pt. 6, pp. 357–442.

Moore, James T. 1982. *Indian and Jesuit: A Seventeenth-Century Encounter.* Chicago: Loyola University Press.

Morgan, Lewis Henry. 1962. *League of the Iroquois.* Secaucus, N.J.: Citadel Press.

Nabokov, Peter. 1967. *Two Leggings: The Making of a Crow Warrior.* New York: Thomas Y. Crowell.

Neihardt, John G. 1972. *Black Elk Speaks: Being the Life Story of a Holy Man of the Oglala Sioux.* New York: Pocket Book Edition.

————. N.d. Ms. fieldnotes for *Black Elk Speaks.* Columbia: University of Missouri Library.

Newcomb, W. W. 1950. "A Re-Examination of the Causes of Plains Warfare." *American Anthropologist* 52 (July–September): 317–30.

Nichols, William. 1983. "Black Elk's Truth." In *Smoothing the Ground: Essays on Native American Oral Literature,* ed. Brian Swann, 334–43. Berkeley: University of California Press.

Nurge, Ethel, ed. 1970. *The Modern Sioux: Social Systems and Reservation Culture.* Lincoln: University of Nebraska Press.

Obrian, Lynn Woods. 1973. *Plains Indian Autobiographies.* Boise State College Western Writers Series, 10. Boise, Idaho: Boise State College.

Oliver, Symmes C. 1962. *Ecology and Cultural Continuity as Contributing Factors in the Social Organization of the Plains Indians.* University of California Publications in American Archeology and Ethnology, vol. 48, no. 1.

Olson, James C. 1965. *Red Cloud and the Sioux Problem.* Lincoln: University of Nebraska Press. See pp. 71–87.

One Feather, Gerald. N.d. *Lakota Wohilikeequapi.* Curriculum Materials Resource Unit, Oglala Sioux Culture Center, Red Cloud Indian School, Pine Ridge, S.D., in cooperation with Black Hills State College, Spearfish, S.D.

Overholt, Thomas W. 1978. "Short Bull, Black Elk, Sword, and the 'Meaning' of the Ghost Dance." In *Religion,* 171–95. Lancaster, Pa.

Parkman, Francis. 1950. *The Oregon Trail.* New York: Signet Classic.

Parssinen, Carol Ann. 1974. "In Pursuit of Ethnography: The Seduction of Science by Art." University of Pennsylvania, Center for Urban Ethnography, Manuscript.

————. 1975. "Paradigms of Ethnographic Realism." Selected Proceedings of the 1975 Conference on Culture and Communication, Working Papers in Culture and Communication, 1:1. Philadelphia: Temple University.

Pearce, Roy Harvey. 1965. *Savagism and Civilization: A Study of the*

Indian and the American Mind. Baltimore: Johns Hopkins University Press.

Perrin, Norman. 1974. *The New Testament: An Introduction.* New York: Harcourt Brace Jovanovich.

Pipes, Nellie B. 1936. "The Protestant Ladder." In *Oregon Historical Quarterly* 37 (September): 237–40.

Powers, William K. 1975. *Oglala Religion.* Lincoln: University of Nebraska Press.

————. 1982. *Yuwipi: Vision and Experience in Oglala Ritual.* Lincoln: University of Nebraska Press.

————. 1990. "When Black Elk Speaks, Everybody Listens." In *Religion in Native North America,* ed. Christopher Vecsey, 135–51. Moscow: University of Idaho Press.

Powers, William K., and Marla N. Powers, 1986. "Putting on the Dog." *Natural History* 95 (no. 2): 6–16.

Proudfoot, Wayne. 1985. *Religious Experience.* Berkeley: University of California Press.

Prucha, Francis Paul. 1988. "Two Roads to Conversion: Protestant and Catholic Missionaries in the Pacific Northwest." *Pacific Northwest Quarterly* 79 (no. 4): 130–37.

Puhl, Louis J. 1963. *The Spiritual Exercises of St. Ignatius.* Westminster, Md.: Newman Press.

Radin, Paul. 1971. *The Trickster: A Study in American Indian Mythology.* New York: Schocken Books.

Rice, Julian. 1991. *Black Elk's Story.* Albuquerque: University of New Mexico Press.

Riegert, Wilbur A. 1975. *Quest for the Pipe of the Sioux.* Rapid City, S.D.

Riggs, Stephen. 1977. *Dakota Grammar, Texts, and Ethnography.* Dept. of the Interior, U.S. Geographical Survey of the Rocky Mountain Region. Reprint. Marvin, S.D.: Blue Cloud Abbey.

Rousseau, Jean-Jacques. 1964. *The First and Second Discourses.* New York: St. Martins Press.

Ruby, Robert H. 1955. *Oglala Sioux.* New York: Vantage Press.

————. 1970. "Yuwipi, Ancient Rite of the Sioux." *Pine Ridge Research Bulletin,* no. 11:20–30.

Sandoz, Mari. 1942. *Crazy Horse: The Strange Man of the Oglalas. A Biography.* Lincoln: University of Nebraska Press.

————. 1961. *These Were the Sioux.* New York: Dell.

Schwarz, O. Douglas. 1981. *Plains Indian Theology: As Expressed in Myth and Ritual and in the Ethics of the Culture.* Ann Arbor, Mich.: University Microfilms International.

Seward, G. 1956. *Psychotherapy and Culture Conflict.* New York: Ronald Press.

Sialm, Placidus. N.d. "Diary." Bureau of Catholic Indian Mission Archives at Marquette University, Milwaukee.

Spier, Leslie. 1921. "The Sun Dance of the Plains Indians: Its Development and Diffusion." *Anthropological Papers of the American Museum of Natural History*, pp. 451–527.

Starkloff, Carl. 1974. *The People of the Center: American Indian Religion and Christianity*. New York: Seabury Press.

Stauffer, Helen. 1981. "Two Authors and a Hero: Neihardt, Sandoz, and Crazy Horse," *Great Plains Quarterly*, Winter, 34–66.

Stedman, Raymond William. 1982. *Shadows of the Indian: Stereotypes in American Culture*. Norman: University of Oklahoma Press.

Steinmetz, Paul B. 1980. *Pipe, Bible, and Peyote among the Oglala Lakota*. Stockholm Studies in Comparative Religion 19. Sweden: Motala. Reprint. Knoxville: University of Tennessee Press, 1990.

Steltenkamp, Michael F. 1982. *The Sacred Vision: Native American Religion and Its Practice Today*. Ramsey, N.J.: Paulist Press.

Stolzman, William. 1974. *Cannunpa Kin: The Pipe, a Position Paper for Common Understanding of Medicine Men and Catholic Pastors*. 3d rev. St. Francis, S.D.

———. 1986. *The Pipe and Christ*. Pine Ridge, S.D.: Red Cloud Indian School.

Talbert, Bob. 1986. "Quotebag." *Detroit Free Press*, June 28.

Taylor, Allan R. 1975. "The Colorado University System for Writing the Lakhota Language." *American Indian Culture and Research Journal* 1:3–12.

Tedlock, Dennis, and Barbara Tedlock. 1975. *Teachings from the American Earth: Indian Religion and Philosophy*. New York: Liveright.

Terrell, John Upton. 1979. *The Arrow and the Cross: A History of the American Indian and the Missionaries*. Santa Barbara, Calif.: Capra Press.

Thwaites, Reuben Gold, ed. 1896. *The Jesuit Relations and Allied Documents: Travels and Exploration of the Jesuit Missionaries in New France, 1610–1791*. 73 vols. Cleveland: Burrows Brs.

Twiss, Gayla, and Eileen Maynard. 1969. *That These People May Live: Conditions among the Oglala Sioux of the Pine Ridge Reservation*. Community Mental Health Program, U.S. Public Health Services, Pine Ridge, S.D.

Two Bulls, Moses. N.d. *Itancan*. Curriculum Materials Resource Unit, Oglala Sioux Culture Center, Red Cloud Indian School, Pine Ridge, S.D. in cooperation with Black Hills State College, Spearfish, S.D.

Utley, Robert M. 1963. *The Last Days of the Sioux Nation*. New Haven: Yale University Press.

Vestal, Stanley. 1932. *Sitting Bull: Champion of the Sioux*. Boston: Houghton Mifflin.

Vogel, Virgil J. 1970. *American Indian Medicine*. Norman: University of Oklahoma Press.

Walker, James R. 1917. "The Sun Dance and Other Ceremonies of the Oglala Division of the Teton Dakota." In American Museum of Natural History, *Anthropological Papers* 16, pt. 2, pp. 50–221. New York.

————. 1980. *Lakota Belief and Ritual*. Edited by Raymond J. DeMallie and Elaine A. Jahner. Lincoln: University of Nebraska Press.

————. 1982. *Lakota Society*. Edited by Raymond J. DeMallie. Lincoln: University of Nebraska Press.

————. 1983. *Lakota Myth*. Edited by Elaine A. Jahner. Lincoln: University of Nebraska Press.

Wallace, Anthony F. C. 1966. *Religion: An Anthropological View*. New York: Random House.

————. 1969. *The Death and Rebirth of the Seneca*. New York: Vantage Books.

Wallis, Wilson D. 1919. *Sun Dance of the Canadian Dakota*. Anthropological Papers of the American Museum of Natural History, vol. 16, Personal Narratives, pp. 317–81. New York: The Trustees.

Waters, Frank. 1984. "Neihardt and the Vision of Black Elk." In *A Sender of Words: Essays in Memory of John G. Neihardt*, ed. Vine Deloria, Jr. Salt Lake City: Howe Brothers.

Willoya, William, and Vinson Brown. 1962. *Warriors of the Rainbow: Strange and Prophetic Dreams of the Indian Peoples*. Healdsburg, Calif.: Naturegraph.

Wind River Rendezvous. 1983. "The Buffalo Culture of the Plains Indians." vol. 13, (April–June) St. Stephens, Wyo.: St. Stephen's Indian Mission Foundation.

Wissler, Clark. 1912. "Societies and Ceremonial Associations in the Oglala Division of the Teton-Dakota." American Museum of Natural History, *Anthropological Papers* 2, pt. 1, pp. 1–99. New York.

Zimmerly, David. 1969. "On Being an Ascetic: Personal Document of a Sioux Medicine Man." *Pine Ridge Research Bulletin*, no. 10:46–69.

Zimmerman, Bill. 1975. *Airlift to Wounded Knee*. Chicago: Swallow Press.

▼

▼

Index

207